"This book offers one hundred brief meditations on Sinatra and his music. Lots of fans out there could write one hundred mash notes, but what makes this book so special is that the fan in question is distinguished poet Lehman, editor of the *Best American Poetry* series and *The Oxford Book of American Poetry*. So expect elegant writing and creative insight along with the outpouring of affection."

—*Library Journal*

"In this set of affectionate and vibrant fan's notes, poet and critic Lehman celebrates Ol' Blue Eyes's hundredth birthday with one hundred impressionistic reflections on the singer's successes and shortcomings. Lehman colorfully points out that Sinatra remains a part of the American cultural scene, with his songs playing in commercials, as background music in restaurants, and in opening and closing credits of movies and television shows such as *Wall Street* and *The Sopranos*. He also has a signature brand of bourbon named after him. Sinatra stays in the public eye, Lehman observes, not only because of his work as a movie actor and a singer but also because of his nonconformity and his fondness for being a maverick. . . . Lehman's lively reflections wonderfully celebrate Sinatra's enduring impact on his own life and on American culture."

—*Publishers Weekly*

"[A] delightful and incisive book. Lehman is a poet, critic, and editor, known for his book on the New York School of poets and *Signs of the Times*. But who would have predicted this tribute to a singer with whom Lehman has had a lifetime love affair? The subtitle, with its crisp pun on 'notes,' takes the singer from his birth in Hoboken in 1915 to his death in Los Angeles in 1998. . . . The notes are pithily, aggressively written, as if to live up to the feisty voice of Lehman's hero, The Voice. He brings out vividly the style of a 'generous, dictatorial, sometimes crude powerful man unafraid to use his power,' which was what the skinny 130-pounder turned into. . . . As always, in talking about a Sinatra recording, Lehman pays attention to minute but significant pleasures the singer brings out. . . . [Lehman] goes further and deeper than Hamill did into what makes Sinatra's treatment of a song so memorable, inimitable."

—William H. Pritchard, *Weekly Standard*

"Threaded through David Lehman's one hundred notes are captivating observations, histories, insights, and reflections likely to serve as interesting dinner party conversations."

—*Beverly Hills Courier*

"I would particularly recommend *Sinatra's Century*, a wonderful new book by the poet, editor, and essayist David Lehman. The book is at once short, fun to dip in and out of, full of quirky yet thoughtful lists of best albums and songs, with a poet's appreciation of Sinatra's craft." —Ken Tucker, Yahoo TV

"His one hundred glowing and gleaming fragments on Sinatra's life and meaning are filled with wildly entertaining quotation, anecdote, and insightful critical judgment. . . . [Lehman is] a gifted critic." —Jeff Simon, *Buffalo News*

"A poet and critic by trade, Lehman has composed a paean that devotes as much space to Sinatra's personality as to his singing. . . . Well-written and unfailingly pleasing to read."

—Terry Teachout, *Commentary*

Sinatra's Century

SINATRA'S CENTURY

ONE HUNDRED NOTES ON

THE MAN AND HIS WORLD

DAVID LEHMAN

HARPER

NEW YORK · LONDON · TORONTO · SYDNEY

HARPER

A hardcover edition of this book was published in 2015 by HarperCollins Publishers.

SINATRA'S CENTURY Copyright © 2015 by David Lehman. All rights reserved. Printed in the United States of America. No part of this book may be used or reproduced in any manner whatsoever without written permission except in the case of brief quotations embodied in critical articles and reviews. For information, address HarperCollins Publishers, 195 Broadway, New York, NY 10007.

HarperCollins books may be purchased for educational, business, or sales promotional use. For information, please e-mail the Special Markets Department at *SPsales@harpercollins.com*.

FIRST HARPER PAPERBACK EDITION PUBLISHED 2016.

Designed by Fritz Metsch

Library of Congress Cataloging-in-Publication Data has been applied for.

ISBN 978-0-06-178007-3 (pbk.)

16 17 18 19 20   OV/RRD   10 9 8 7 6 5 4 3 2 1

For Amy Gerstler

There's an old French saying,
"the whole of a man's mystery
rests in his hat," and if you
translate it into American
you get Sinatra smoking
and singing "Memories of
You," "I Thought About You,"
"You Make Me Feel So Young,"
and "You Brought a New
Kind of Love to Me," all
from the same 1956 session,
I love that voice and have since
the summer I was eight and
my friend Ann and I sang "Love
and Marriage" on Talent Night
at the bungalow colony when I'm
down there's nothing like you,
birthday boy, singing "All of Me"
to lift me up and when I'm in love
I jump out of bed in the morning
singing "It All Depends On You" and
your voice comes out of my mouth

May you live to be a hundred,
and may the last voice you hear be mine.

— F S

Sinatra's Century

Michael Ochs Archives / Getty Images

(1)

AT ZITO'S BAKERY on Bleecker Street, a Greenwich Village landmark for eighty years before it closed its doors in 2004, customers saw two framed photographs on the wall behind the counter. One was a picture of the pope. The other was a picture of Frank Sinatra.

(2)

DIRECTLY AFTER EVERY baseball game at Yankee Stadium, the public address system plays Sinatra's signature recording of Kander and Ebb's "New York, New York." When the Yankees defeated the Atlanta Braves in the sixth and final game of the 1996 World Series, capping an improbable comeback from a two-games-to-none deficit, it seemed as if everyone in the stadium was singing along, swelling the final chorus: "And if I can make it there, I can make it anywhere / It's up to you, New York, New York." The aging Sinatra—he was in his sixties when he recorded "New York, New York," the last of his blockbuster hits—does amazing things with that initial *And*, twisting and turning the word as if it contained not one but three or four syllables; the voice seems to go down a valley and come back up the other side of a hill. The gesture is inimitable, though it also invites imitation, and watching a Sinatra fan trying to duplicate the effect can be very entertaining. But here the voice was the instrument of joyous release. Here you had a crowd of almost sixty thousand people getting into the act. It was a great moment of New York solidarity, and it was also, in its way, an expression of Frankophilia: the populace's love affair with the greatest of all popular American singers.

Triumphal, assertive, and endowed with civic pride, the hymn to the city that doesn't sleep is New York's official song. John Kander and Fred Ebb, who had previously given us the

score of *Cabaret*, wrote "New York, New York" for Liza Minnelli to belt out in Martin Scorsese's 1977 movie of the same
title, with Minnelli as a vocalist on the rise and Robert De
Niro as the saxophone player she meets in a New York nightclub on V-J Day in 1945. Once upon a decade, the Yankees
played Minnelli's rendition of "New York, New York" after
a loss and Sinatra's after a win. Liza protested and now, win
or lose, it is Frank's version that you hear after every game at
Yankee Stadium.

The song has become the city's anthem. There was always
competition for the distinction; New York is, after all, the
home of Tin Pan Alley, Broadway, and some of the country's
most celebrated cabarets, clubs, and performance spaces. "The
Sidewalks of New York" was the city's early-century anthem,
played by the band at the end of *Sunrise at Campobello* when a
polio-stricken Franklin Roosevelt makes his way to the lectern
to nominate Alfred E. Smith at the 1924 Democratic National
Convention. "Manhattan," Rodgers and Hart's breakout hit,
caused a sensation when the first audience heard it at the *Gar-
rick Gaieties of 1925*. Hart's sophisticated and witty lyric—in
which pleasures are praised according to their affordability—
salutes not only Chinatown's Mott Street and Central Park but
the Bronx, Staten Island, Coney Island (where we'll eat balo-
ney sandwiches), and even Yonkers (where true love conquers
all). Before Kander and Ebb, Leonard Bernstein wrote a song
called "New York, New York," with lyrics by Betty Comden
and Adolph Green, for *On the Town* (1944). The song kicks off
the story with a madcap burst of energy: three U. S. sailors are
on shore leave for twenty-four romantic hours in a "helluva"
town (the original Broadway show) or a "wonderful" town

With the cast of *On The Town*.

Michael Ochs Archives / Getty Images

(Hollywood's rephrasing)—a place where people "ride in a hole in the ground," though even in the subway you will see women decked out in "silk and satin" and everyone's up for a date. There are other wonderful songs that glorify one aspect or another of the city: "Take the A Train," "Lullaby of Broadway," "Lullaby of Birdland," "Manhattan Serenade." But as a theme that doubles as a fight song, Kander and Ebb's "New York, New York" is top of the list, king of the hill, and it is the Sinatra version that defines the way New Yorkers see themselves and their beloved, if sometimes embattled, city.

Few men—and fewer nonathletes—know what it feels like to bring sixty thousand cheering people to their feet. Sinatra had that power. It was (and still is) his voice that thousands of men hear coming out of their mouths in the shower. At Columbia Lions basketball games, the college band plays "Roar, Lion, Roar" at regular intervals, but when the game against Harvard or Princeton has ended and the Ivy League crowd heads toward the exits, the familiar voice comes over the loudspeaker and *starts spreadin' the news*. At Chicago's United Center, where the Bulls of Michael Jordan held court, and which Sinatra officially opened with one of his last live concerts, it is "My Kind of Town" that is played—the song Jimmy Van Heusen and Sammy Cahn wrote to order for their boss's last singing picture, *Robin and the Seven Hoods* in 1964. In the Chicago Cubs' venerable Wrigley Field, it is "Chicago (That Toddlin' Town)" that you may sometimes hear between innings or after the game. In each case it is not just the song itself, but Sinatra's rendition, that is accepted as definitive.

ON DECEMBER 12, 2015, Frank Sinatra turns one hundred. Fans need no reason beyond the occasion for a songfest—or a Festschrift—but there are a number of serious arguments I would put forward in the course of a celebration.

The first is that Sinatra continues to figure in at least three aesthetic realms: as a singer, as a movie actor and movie star, and as an almost mythic personage about whom hundreds of thousands of words have been written. There remains something new to be said about Sinatra's singular claim on our attention—his "image," an image that evolved so extraordinarily in the course of his career. To an aficionado, and there are plenty, Sinatra, as he would be taken, "a man and his music," is an aesthetic experience of intense pleasure, which grows only greater when shared among friends.

Sinatra is a brand. On Sirius XM satellite radio, "Siriusly Sinatra" features Sinatra above all, with whole programs devoted to him (*The Chairman's Hour*). Daughter Nancy hosts a regular show (*Nancy for Frank*), and there are occasional features with her siblings, Frank Jr. and Tina. But the brand extends to other singers, whose covers of classic American popular songs are regularly played on the station. Here is a partial list: Eydie Gorme, Steve Lawrence (to whom FS willed the arrangements of his repertory of songs), Vic Damone, Tony Bennett, Bing Crosby, Judy Garland, Johnny Mercer, Ella Fitzgerald, Jack Jones, Mel Tormé, Jo Stafford, Peggy Lee,

Rosemary Clooney, Bobby Darin, Dinah Washington, Fred Astaire, Joe Williams, Lena Horne, Johnny Hartman, June Christy, Jimmy Durante, Bobby Short, Gene Kelly, Nancy Wilson, Nina Simone, Perry Como, Barbra Streisand, Nat (King) Cole, Louis Armstrong, Doris Day, Sammy Davis, Jr., Dean Martin, Dinah Shore, Sarah Vaughan, Billie Holiday, Willie Nelson, Michael Bublé, Eva Cassidy, Joanie Sommers, Kenny Rankin, Diane Schuur, Linda Ronstadt, Bette Midler, Diana Krall, Sue Raney, Robbie Williams, Tony DeSare, Madeleine Peyroux. Guest hosts "playing favorites" include Liza Minnelli, Johnny Mathis, Freddy Cole, Julius La Rosa, Carly Simon, Julie Budd, Dana Delany, and Melissa Manchester.

Right now, as I write this (August 1, 2014), Mitzi Gaynor is the disc jockey on duty, and Mitzi, who played Martha, the chorus girl who married Joe E. Lewis (Sinatra), in *The Joker Is Wild* (1957), naturally plays the big hit from that movie, "All the Way." What other Sinatra songs will she play? "Nancy (with the Laughing Face)," "Fly Me to the Moon," Jimmy Van Heusen's "Here's That Rainy Day." Biggest surprise: she closes with "I Couldn't Sleep a Wink Last Night," which a young Frankie sings with an a cappella chorus, because the instrumentalists were on strike that year, 1943.

And here, taking over the microphone, is Robert Wagner, who traveled with FS and was a pallbearer at his funeral. He plays "No One Cares," "The Lady Is a Tramp" ("great arrangement!"), and "The Way You Look Tonight." Wagner tells us he is married to the glamorous Jill St. John, who, if I hear him correctly, had been Frank's date when the guys double-dated back in the day. Wagner's date was Frank's daughter, Tina.

Sinatra is both genus and species of the brand, whose currency is invaluable to one who believes in the greatness of the

classic American popular song—the songs of Kern, the Gersh-
wins, Berlin, Rodgers & Hart, Rodgers & Hammerstein,
Lerner & Loewe, Harold Arlen with Yip Harburg or Johnny
Mercer or Ted Koehler, Arthur Schwartz with Howard Dietz,
Walter Donaldson with Gus Kahn, Leonard Bernstein with
Betty Comden and Adolph Green, Frank Loesser, Doro-
thy Fields, Leo Robin, Gus Kahn, Hoagy Carmichael, Harry
Warren, Vincent Youmans, Arthur Freed, Peggy Lee, Stephen
Sondheim, Cy Coleman, Carolyn Leigh, and way too many
worthy others to fit into this overstuffed sentence. Sinatra and
company have kept this music alive, kept it from slipping into
the museums.

The second argument is that Sinatra remains of the moment.
You will hear him in commercials for vodka or sour mash whiskey, as segue music on radio and television, as the background
music in the restaurant with steak and chops on the menu and a
full bar, as the music in your head, as the song playing over the
movie's opening credits (*This Boy's Life*, *Wall Street*) or closing
credits (*Summer of Sam*, *Executive Decision*). Given the fickle-
ness of audiences—and, too, the prevalence of a culture that is
largely indifferent to the popular music of Sinatra's heyday—
the longevity of the Sinatra brand is pretty amazing.

The third argument is that Sinatra's enduring fame reflects
not only his accomplishments as a singer but his assertion of
himself. He was a one-of-a-kind, a maverick, the ultimate
nonconformist, and as such a monument to Emersonian self-
reliance. There is something to be gained by considering
Sinatra in the context of our evolving modern ideas of what
constitutes manhood, manliness, masculinity. He was strongly
ethnic, the son of Italian immigrants, a working-class hero.
He championed tolerance and at the same time violated every

tenet of political correctness before that phrase entered the lexicon. He never tired of jesting about race, religion, sex, and ethnic identity—including his own. Sometimes at a concert, for a laugh, he would take a phrase in a song and render it in a greenhorn's exaggerated accent: "The British museum had losea da charm," for example, in "A Foggy Day (in London Town)." But his ethnic pride was unquestionable, and he was, inevitably, asked to serve as chairman of the American Italian Anti-Defamation League in 1967. (He resigned when, just as inevitably, the appointment provoked controversy.)

It is neither incidental nor accidental that he became a favorite son in the Italian-American community. And that would be because, and not in spite of, his solidarity with gangland's wise guys. It may have outraged the columnists and a sector of public opinion, but the sociologist Daniel Bell understood the phenomenon, observing, in his 1953 essay "Crime As an American Way of Life," that "To the world at large, the news and pictures of Frank Sinatra, for example, mingling with former Italian mobsters could come somewhat as a shock. Yet to Sinatra, and to many Italians, these were men who had grown up in their neighborhood and who were, in some instances, bywords in the community for their helpfulness and their charities."

It is beyond dispute that the men of the mob had a soft spot for him. And that fondness went both ways. Eddie Fisher remembers hearing Sinatra say that he'd "rather be a don for the Mafia than President of the United States." "I think that he's always nurtured a secret desire to be a 'hood,' " Bing Crosby told a *Cosmopolitan* writer in 1956. "But, of course, he has too much class, too much sense, to go that route—so he gets his kicks out of barking at newsmen and so forth." Shirley MacLaine: "Sinatra has always loved gangsters in a romantic,

theatrical way, as though he wanted to be one." Peter Lawford: "Frank idolized [Sam Giancana] because he was the Mafia's top gun. Frank loved to talk about 'hits' and guys getting
'rubbed out.' "

Not everyone was willing to smile indulgently, look the
other way, or cower at the hoodlum side of the singer's personality. In 1947, columnist Robert Ruark of the Scripps-
Howard chain, his voice dripping with disdain, broke the story
that Sinatra was hanging out with Lucky Luciano in Havana.
Ruark seized the occasion to knock the singer's leftist politics.
"This curious desire to cavort among the scum is possibly per-
missible among citizens who are not peddling sermons to the
nation's youth and may even be allowed to a mealy-mouthed
celebrity if he is smart enough to confine his social tolerance to
a hotel room," Ruark lectured. As the journalist saw it, it was
as if Sinatra's behavior invalidated "his movie shorts on tolerance, and his frequent dabblings into the do-good department
of politics." So much for *The House I Live In* (1945), the moving
ten-minute short promoting religious tolerance, which won an
Academy Award. Like everyone else who worked on that ide-
alistic film, Frank provided his services free of charge. In 1985,
the cartoonist Garry Trudeau let Sinatra have it in a series of
Doonesbury strips in which a goggle-eyed Frank collapses in
hero worship when he meets mobsters: "Made guys? You're all
murderers? Wow! No kidding?"

That Sinatra continued to project vulnerability, as a singer
and as an actor, is all the more remarkable since in his public
persona he evolved from the shy teen idol of the early years
to the top dog, the boss, the man-about-town who had only to
snap his fingers to make cars, planes, flunkies appear, eager to
do his bidding. Sinatra was an avatar of style. He took care of

O'Neill / Getty Images

his appearance in the time-honored manner of *la bella figura*, the Italian ideal requiring one to dress impeccably and handle any situation gracefully—or, in Sinatra's terms, with class. The various accoutrements he favored all gained by their association with him. In the 1940s, those boyish bow ties; in the 1950s and after, the snap-brim fedora, and perhaps a belted raincoat to sling over one shoulder; the tuxedo in the casino at night ("For me," he said, "a tuxedo is a way of life"); the cigarette; the glass of whiskey; the lamppost he could lean against while he smoked and sang. These are all aspects of the phenomenon and are not to be underrated. That fetishized cigarette, especially. It's a drug, a vehicle for escape, but it is also a little torch that burns. The smoke of Frank's cigarette curls in the air when, in the wee small hours, he sings "Deep in a Dream" (music, Jimmy Van Heusen; lyrics, Eddie DeLange). The smoke creates the mirage of a stairway, and down the stairs the lady descends. But the bliss lasts no longer than a dream, it being a condition of such visions that they refuse to stay. "My cigarette burns me, I wake with a start / My hand isn't hurt, but there's a pain in my heart."

And then there is the part of his narrative that accentuates the negative, the same way that the great songwriters tended to gravitate to the minor key. Sinatra is a noir hero. He reminds you that he can fail, has failed, has "done his share of losing," and has the right to sing the blues. Here's that rainy day. You can't forget her—soon you even stop trying. In the early 1960s, when Frank was riding high, he lifted his glass and sang "Here's to the Losers." Sample line: "Here's to those who drink their dinner when that lady doesn't show." In 1974, at Sinatra's request, Tom Adair wrote a new set of lyrics for the song Adair and composer Matt Dennis crafted more than three decades earlier: "Everything Happens to Me." In a 1981 recording of the song—Nancy Sinatra (Frank's daughter) played it the other night on her satellite radio show—Frank rasps that "in the school of life," when he was "lucky just to pass," he found himself "chasing rainbows with the losers in the class." We believe the stuff about losing—we know he's been there—though in another part of our consciousness he is dancing with Ava Gardner, on top of the world, whispering in her ear, "Every cat in here wants to be me, and every chick wants to be you."

The fourth argument is an extension of the third. It is that in Sinatra's career you see the cultural history of America in the twentieth century—the strange winding journey from Prohibition and the Depression to prosperity and its discontents on the other side of global war and terror on an unprecedented scale.

4

WE WERE AT the Argos, on East State Street in Ithaca, New York, drinking Bagpipe Mariachis (Espolón Blanco tequila, house-made apple-fennel shrub, lemon, and house-made celery bitters, topped off with Laphroaig scotch with its distinctively smoky flavor). I said I was writing a book on Sinatra and my friend said, "What are you going to say?" Or maybe she asked, "What do you think he stands for?"

The next seven hundred words are for her.

What does Sinatra stand for? Above all, genius as a singer and performer. He had the ability to give a song its definitive exposition, even to make it seem like an extension of his own personality and experience. Excellence of *phrasing* is the consensus regarding his spot-on musical timing. His respect for the meaning of a lyric is matched by his intuitive grasp of the melodic and harmonic possibilities.

To this, add the fascination of a larger-than-life personality. The ambitious, driven hero of an irresistible show-biz comeback narrative, Sinatra was also an "eighteen-karat manic depressive," a wounded swinger who could consort with gangsters but also liked to paint, won a Grammy for album design, took quality photographs of a ballyhooed prizefight for *Life*, and treated a popular song written for the masses as if it were a sonnet meant for patrician ears. The stages in Sinatra's life correspond to the fluctuations in our climate of cultural opinion. The trajectory of his career extended from Roosevelt to Reagan, from the big band era (which he took part in but also helped bring to an end by going solo successfully in 1942) to beyond the Las Vegas casino scene of the go-go 1960s. He went nightclubbing with JFK, performed at the Nixon White House, took tea regularly with Nancy Reagan when her husband was commander in chief. Before all that, he had participated in the common citizen's love of FDR. When he sings the great Vernon Duke and Ira Gershwin standard "I Can't Get Started" on the album *No One Cares* (1959), Ira provided him with some superb new lyrics, including this couplet: "Each time I chanced to see Franklin D. / He always said, 'Hi, buddy,' to me," which Sinatra sings with glamorous melancholy.

In his twenties, Sinatra boxed to keep in shape, so I'll use pugilistic argot to describe the transformative sequence of events in his career. He led with a jab, scored with a combination, clinched, absorbed punishing body blows, took an uppercut to the chin. He was ahead on points when a left hook decked him in the next round. When he staggered to his feet at the count of eight, his handlers were ready to throw in the towel. But then, against all odds, he picked himself up, took a deep breath, and knocked out his opponent. You can't beat that on the masculinity meter. Some people who never met him worship him. Some people were scared shitless of the guy. Frank's daughter Nancy, with whom he sang the top-of-the-charts hit "Somethin' Stupid" in the late 1960s, said that trying to define him was like trying to analyze electricity.

The contradictions hit you like a Marciano right. Debbie Reynolds, who costarred with him in *The Tender Trap*, said, "If

Getting a workout.

Herbert Gehr / Getty Images

he liked you it was forever, and if he disliked you—I wouldn't want to be there." Sinatra was a great friend who could behave with grace and courage. He could also act like a jerk with a bad case of the entitlement blues, and could hold on to a grudge until the twelfth of never. An incurable romantic, he fell in love too easily and too fast, but also referred to women as "broads" and acted sometimes as if the battle of the sexes were a constant, but, luckily, sleeping with the enemy was encouraged. He was generous, dictatorial, sometimes crude, a powerful man unafraid to use his power. He couldn't fall asleep, couldn't stand being alone, had supreme self-confidence, and was spoiled by fate and fame. He had about the speediest metabolism you can imagine, an impatience of epic proportions, and an evil temper. When he lost it big-time, it was ugly and made news. His caprices were like royal edicts. If you were in his circle, you might get a phone call at any hour advising you to be ready to take a flight on his private jet to Vegas, or wherever Frank felt like flying.

You know the Dos Equis TV commercial in which a man reeking of *savoir faire* is said to be "the most interesting man in the world"? I always thought it should be "the most interesting man in the room." Frank Sinatra was the most interesting man in the world.

In 1938, Frank was charged with "carrying on with a married woman."

Michael Ochs Archives / Getty Images

5

ON JUNE 26, 2014, Sinatra's first New Jersey driver's license went for $15,757, according to Boston-based auction house RR Auction. The license was dated 1934; the boy was listed as nineteen. He was still living with his parents at 841 Garden Street in Hoboken, New Jersey, not far from his Monroe Street childhood home. He was born there, in that house, on December 12, 1915, a big baby at thirteen and a half pounds, requiring forceps and showing the marks of a difficult birth for as long as he lived: a lacerated ear, scars on the left side of his face. According to the license, Sinatra the young man was five foot eight and weighed one hundred and thirty pounds. The auction lot included a 1940 letter to New Jersey's Commissioner of Motor Vehicles, sent by a lawyer representing a man who survived a car crash with Sinatra. He insisted that the young man's license be suspended until he paid for damages. That was a couple of years after Frank's first well-documented brush with the law—in November 1938, when the Bergen County sheriff's office charged him with the attempted "seduction" of a married woman. The mug shot of Arrest #42799, head and profile, appears nowadays on posters around the world.

The juvenile delinquent—or "juve delinq," to use the lingo of newspaper columnist Lee Mortimer, a constant thorn in Sinatra's hide—was one disguise favored by the lonely boy whose face showed scars of his difficult birth. They called him "Scarface." Other youthful nicknames were "Bones" (because he was skinny), "Slacksey" (because of the many pairs of trousers his doting mother bought for him), and "Angles" (because of his penchant for smart-ass pranks).* He was a decent athlete, a strong swimmer. In the boxing ring he had fast hands. He did his best to look dapper. From the start he was a neat freak. Even as an adult, when he smoked ceaseless packs of unfiltered Camels, he couldn't stand the sight of an ashtray filled with butts. His habit of frequently washing his hands prompted musicians to joke about his "Lady Macbeth routine."

Sinatra's father (born in Sicily) was a former bantamweight who boxed under the name Marty O'Brien, the prejudice against the Irish at that time being less severe than that leveled at recently arrived Italian-Americans like Anthony Martin Sinatra. It was for the likes of them that "wops"—the slur deriving from the Neapolitan term for "thug" though sometimes considered shorthand for "without papers"—entered the lexicon. When Martin Sinatra, who suffered from asthma, was too old to box or work on the docks, strings were pulled and he got work as a firefighter. Sinatra loved his father, and the old man's death in 1969 contributed to the son's short-lived decision to retire in 1971.

But it was Sinatra's mother, Dolly, who loomed larger than life in his consciousness. Dolly had a big personality. Born in Genoa, she became a player in local Hoboken politics, a Democratic Party fixer, despite a reputation for selling illegal booze

---

*On "Angles," see Anthony Summer and Robbyn Swan, *Sinatra: The Life* (New York: Knopf, 2005), p. 23. "Angles" fits for more reasons than one: he remained a prankster as an adult, tossing off cherry bombs. But the word comes to mind also because of his angular face as a young man, his lanky, angular frame, and his line about how to wear a fedora: "Cock your hats," he said. "Angles are attitudes."

With his early vocal group, the Hoboken Four.

Hulton Archive / Getty Images

and performing illegal abortions. It was she who pulled those strings that got her husband a good secure city job. If you want to understand Sinatra, you had better begin with the fact that he was an only son and that his mother was a domineering personality who practiced tough love, put her son in his place ("Mr. Big Shot"), swore like a sailor, alternately spoiled and neglected him, expected great things from him, nixed romances that she considered unsuitable, and was furious when he dropped out of A. J. Demarest High School after only forty-seven days. It was from her that he inherited his hot temper, and from her that he internalized the determination to succeed.

Neither parent thought Frank had any future as a singer. When the young man set his heart on becoming a singer, Sinatra's father reacted with the tersest and perhaps most devastating bit of music criticism on record: "Get out." Get out of the house. Get a job. Be a man. Get rid of your illusions. Dolly Sinatra said much the same thing: "If you think you're going to be a goddamned loafer, you're crazy."

Sinatra couldn't wait to get out of Hoboken and hop the ferry to New York. Years later, when he mentions Hoboken in a recording session with his pals Dean Martin and Sammy Davis, it made for an easy laugh—shorthand for the place you don't want to be if you're Frank Sinatra. But Hoboken doesn't mind. Go to Leo's, also known as Leo's Grandevous, a restaurant in the heart of Hoboken, near the street where Frank was born. Take in the scores of black-and-white photos on the wall of fame, and listen to the voice on the jukebox. The menu in this shrine to Sinatra's memory is traditional Italian, and there's a full bar in the shape of a half moon.

Dolly Sinatra, herself a feisty embodiment of Hoboken civic pride, delivered her opinions with authority all her life. During

World War II, she was furious with President Roosevelt for calling the Italians "a lot of opera singers" and a less dangerous foe than the Germans. In 1944, when Frank failed to come back to Hoboken to help his mother with a political campaign, she scolded him: "But you campaigned for that Roosevelt!"

In January 1977, a private plane was carrying Mama Sinatra from Palm Springs to Las Vegas, transporting her and a friend to Frank's opening-night performance at Caesars Palace, when it crashed en route. Dolly died in the crash.

But in her son's consciousness, Dolly retained her force as a font of opinion and judgment.

"She scared the shit outta me," Sinatra told Shirley Mac-Laine.

In 1998, when he lay dying, Sinatra had a designated thug in his room at all times. At one point Sinatra raised his head and pointed to an empty armchair. "Could you get my mother out of here?" he said. "I'm trying to get some rest, but she keeps hanging around."

With Ava Gardner and his parents.

New York Daily News Archive / Getty Images

(6)

THE SHREWDEST SINGLE sentence in Kitty Kelley's book on Sinatra, *His Way*, is this quotation from Freud in the context of the mutual antipathy between Frank and Lyndon Johnson, two boys whose mothers adored them. Freud wrote, "A man who has been the indisputable favorite of his mother keeps for life the feeling of a conqueror, that confidence of success that often induces real successes."*

---

*Freud recorded this observation in a short essay on Goethe, "A Childhood Recollection from *Dichtung und Wahrheit*," which appears—in a somewhat different translation from the one Kitty Kelley consulted—in Freud, *Character and Culture*, ed. Philip Rieff (New York: Collier Books, 1963), pp. 191–201.

Onstage with Harry James.

CBS Photo Archive / Getty Images

"EVERYTHING'S MOVIN' TOO fast," Peggy Lee sang, though for Sinatra it wasn't nearly fast enough. In 1939 he began the year as a singing waiter at the Rustic Cabin, on the Jersey side of the George Washington Bridge, near Englewood. In the decades since, maybe a million people claim to have heard him perform there. One person who did hear Sinatra sing at the Rustic Cabin was Harry James, he of the mustache and magnificent trumpet. According to Helen Forrest, who excelled as the band's girl singer in its glory days but made the mistake of falling in love with the bandleader, who jilted her, the photogenic James was so thin he "made Frank look fat." Two years older than Sinatra, and taller, James had left Benny Goodman's band to form a new one of his own. In two years' time, with the band's "You Made Me Love You" on the top ten list, Harry James and his Music Makers would rank among the best and most popular big bands. Dick Haymes would succeed Sinatra as the band's boy singer; Buddy Rich would play drums. (Rich considered himself the Ted Williams of drummers.)* But in 1939 the James band was just getting started, and when he signed Sinatra, the best Harry could offer was a one-year contract at $75 a week.

*Williams was evidently the standard. Dave Frishberg, who worked with Zoot Sims, says he told Sims that "if [Al] Cohn was the Joe DiMaggio of tenor saxophonists, he [Sims] was the Ted Williams." Whitney Balliett, *American Musicians: 56 Portraits in Jazz* (New York: Oxford University Press, 1986), p. 276; see p. 234 for the Buddy Rich quote.

"When Frank joined the band," James remarked, "he was always thinking of the lyrics. The melody was secondary. If it was a delicate or pretty word, he would try to phrase it with a prettier, softer type of voice. . . . He could sing the wrong melody, and it would still be pretty."

With the James band, Sinatra sang "It's Funny to Everyone but Me" in early August. When he started singing, Sinatra wrote in a "Me and My Music" article in *Life* magazine in 1965, "everybody was trying to copy the Crosby style—the casual kind of raspy sound in the throat. Bing was on top, and a bunch of us— Dick Todd, Bob Eberly, Perry Como, and Dean Martin—were trying to break in. It occurred to me that maybe the world didn't need another Crosby. I decided to experiment a little and come up with something different. What I finally hit on was more the *bel canto* Italian school of singing, without making a point of it. That meant I had to stay in better shape because I had to sing more. It was more difficult than Crosby's style, much more difficult." Hallmarks of *bel canto* style, all of which apply to Sinatra, include clear enunciation of each word, with no syllable lost; the ability to soften a high note ("to avoid screaming"), to "glide with the vowels," and to move "gently" from higher to lower notes; no repetition without variation; and mastery of "how to steal the time in singing" (that is, tempo rubato, the secret art of phrasing).

Sinatra, Pete Hamill writes, "created a new model for American masculinity," and this was apparent from the start. So was the singer's countervailing confidence, even defiance. James wanted his new boy singer to change his name to "Frankie Satin." Fuck that. His mother would kill him. He was Frank Sinatra, and he would stay that way. Years later, when asked about the proposed name change, Sinatra cracked, "If I'd done that, I'd be working cruise ships today."

8

THE EARLY EVIDENCE might not have suggested that Sinatra's posthumous destiny would be so prolific, although even in his earliest records he was shrewd enough to sing not only new songs but what we have come to call "standards": the Gershwins' "Embraceable You," Berlin's "How Deep Is the Ocean," Porter's "Night and Day," Kern's "The Song Is You," Arlen's "Stormy Weather," Vincent Youmans's "Without a Song," Rube Bloom's "Fools Rush In" (with the Johnny Mercer lyric that opens with an Alexander Pope epigram: "Fools rush in where angels fear to tread"). Capable of crossing the northern border into tenor territory, with violins in sweet support, his youthful baritone bewitched a generation of teenage girls. They made an art out of swooning at the Paramount Theater in Times Square, where a Sinatra appearance filled the seats and caused mayhem around the block outside. Time has vindicated the taste of the bobby-soxers—the girls who were known by the ankle-length socks they wore—who shrieked with joy in 1943 and '44, started fan clubs with funny names (the Subjects of the Sultan of Swoon, the Bow-tie-dolizers, the Frank Sinatra Fan and Mah-Jongg Club), and thought, to a girl, that the frail-looking lad onstage hugging the microphone, Frankie of the hollow cheeks, was singing *to her* when he sang "You'll Never Know" or "I've Got a Crush on You."*

---

*When a school gymnasium was used as a dance floor, the kids would have to take off their shoes. Thus, the "sock hop."

Mobbed by fans in Pasadena.

Hulton Archive / Getty Images

Sinatra was the big band era's boy singer par excellence. And there are some who prefer the timbre of his youthful voice—among them his granddaughter, A. J. Lambert. Nancy's daughter devoted the July 2014 edition of her satellite radio program, *Third Generation*, to the music of Richard Rodgers and played a rare recording of Sinatra singing "If I Loved You"(from *Carousel*) in the 1940s. His voice is creamy, capable of amazing softness, tenderness, reaching the Everest of high notes without strain. A hallmark of Jerome Kern's songs is that they soar, and you can't beat what the young Sinatra does with classic Kern ballads such as "The Song Is You" (the closing falsetto note is beyond credible) and "All the Things You Are" (lovely what he does at the end of the bridge), again, in the 1940s.

Of the ingredients of a great singer—vocal power, range, and tone; phrasing; enunciation; style; dramatic intensity and rhetorical power—it was the singular purity of his voice and its extraordinary range that earned him the first of his nicknames: *the Voice*. The famous phrasing would come later, though we had intimations of it from the start. He grasped instinctively the principle that Yip Harburg stated in an interview with Gene Lees: "Words make you think thoughts. Music makes you feel a feeling. But a song can make you feel a thought."*

I would argue that one other element distinguished Sinatra from the other elegant baritones of the period. He sounded more like a boy than any of them.

---

*To "feel a thought": Harburg sounds almost like T. S. Eliot describing the metaphysical poets of the seventeenth-century (Donne, Marvell, et al.). See "The Squirrel" in Gene Lees, *Singers and the Song II* (New York: Oxford University Press, 1998), p. 45.

9

SINATRA LOVED THE two bands he sang with, Harry James's in 1939 and Tommy Dorsey's for the next two and a half years. In the 1960s, two decades after the big band era had run its course, he relished the opportunity to sing with Count Basie's big band, which had somehow survived. On one TV special, after he un-retired in 1973, he assembled a fifty-four-piece orchestra with twenty violins.

Given his love of the big band sound and his insistence on singing with a live orchestra (as opposed to overdubbing in a studio), it is ironic that when Sinatra left Tommy Dorsey's band for a solo career in 1942, it spelled the beginning of the end of the big band era. A ruinous musicians' strike, sidelining the instrumentalists for the last months of 1942 and all of 1943, delivered the knockout punch. Henceforth the attention shifted from a band of multiple musicians with a leader to the individual singer or singing group supported by a band of whatever size.

The standard big band was built on a foundation of seventeen musicians: five saxophones, four trumpets, four trombones, and a four-piece rhythm section—*plus* voices, *plus* flutes, clarinets, strings, banjo, French horn, or whatever other instruments the band leader favored. You could have, say, thirty-two pieces, led by pianist Bill Miller, if you were Frank Sinatra at the Copa Room of the Sands Hotel in Vegas in 1990.

A big band recording usually began with an instrumental chorus followed by a vocal chorus and sometimes a half chorus of instrumental going out. A featured instrumental-ist played the melody on his clarinet (Benny Goodman, Artie Shaw), trombone (Dorsey), trumpet (James), for the first run-through. The voice or voices were held in reserve for the second chorus. There was a chance for the brass section to shine, or the pianist, the hotshot drummer, the boy singer, the girl singer, the vocal group. The voice was only one element—important, but not more important than, say, Bunny Berigan's trumpet, Woody Herman's clarinet, Jack Teagarden's trombone, Lionel Hampton's vibes, Lester Young's tenor sax, or Teddy Wilson's piano.

Form followed function, the function of the band being to play music the young people could dance to—and in those days everybody danced. After all, dancing was, in a quip attributed to Shaw (George Bernard, not Artie), "the perpendicular expression of a horizontal desire."

But then everything changed.

A fifteen-year-old Montreal girl on her first date—a dance to the sounds of the Tommy Dorsey Orchestra—recalls just what happened when the skinny boy singer sang a ballad: "The dancing stopped." He made her feel those magic words: "He's singing to *me*."* When the dancers stopped dancing and gathered around the singer to listen, the change was monumental. The singing became the main event, not just part of the prompt for dancing.

The Dorsey band, in songs like "Let's Get Away from It

---

*And ever after she "was pleased and proud if the press wrote nice things about him, and embarrassed when the reports were bad. It was as if a family member had misbehaved." Shirley M. Kelley, "Memories of Sinatra" in *Legend*, ed. Ethlie Ann Vare (New York: Boulevard Books, 1995), p. 43.

With Tommy Dorsey.

Michael Ochs Archives / Getty Images

All," experimented with letting the voice, or voices, take the lead. A chorus sung by the Pied Pipers, anchored by Jo Stafford, preceded a duet of Sinatra and Connie Haines. Soon enough the exception became the rule, with the inevitable result that the singer was promoted, and the bandleader and solo instrumentalists correspondingly demoted, in the musical hierarchy. Fans soon understood that Ella Fitzgerald's existence did not depend on the Chick Webb band, and the same was true for other big band singers, such as Doris Day (who had sung with Les Brown "and His Band of Renown"), Peggy Lee (with Benny Goodman), Dick Haymes and Helen Forrest (with Harry James), Billie Holiday (with Count Basie and Artie Shaw), and Anita O'Day (with Stan Kenton).

Mel Tormé summed up the change: "Frank's rise to fame ushered in a new era in popular music—a vocalist's era." History had identified itself with Frank Sinatra.

It astounds me that the reign of the big bands, which left us so rich and enduring a musical legacy, lasted a mere twenty years or so. An even more incredible fact about the great music America produced in the 1930s and forties was its mass popularity. You turned on the radio and there it was.

The big bands had begun to decline by the time I was born, and as I never knew the real thing, I feel free to idealize an occupation that promised a talented young man with a horn some limited amount of glory, good companionship, long hours but no job security living out of a suitcase in drab hotels and killing time by playing cards. Though the work of performing the dance music of the day was no hardship, going by bus from town to town was an ordeal entailing hours of boredom and discomfort. The pay was crummy, the boss usually a lout, and yet the musicians looked back with fondness on the era after it was gone, some of them even dreaming of a big band of their own. Lester Young, the tenor saxophonist whose nickname among jazz musicians was "Pres" (as in President), used to say that his ideal big band would have Sinatra and Jo Stafford as his boy and girl singers.*

*Lester Young called Billie Holiday "Lady Day" and she returned the favor by calling him "Pres." She said that Lester was to the saxophone what President Roosevelt was to the nation. See Gary Giddins, *Weather Bird: Jazz at the Dawn of Its Second Century* (New York: Oxford University Press, 2004), p. 358. See also Lees, *Singers and the Song II*, p. 118.

10

BANDLEADER ARTIE SHAW, master of the clarinet, whose version of "Begin the Beguine" beguiled Americans in the 1940s, was Sinatra's predecessor as Ava Gardner's husband. The odd fact intimates a point worth reiterating. When Sinatra arrived on the scene, the bandleader was the most glamorous position in the music world. I think immediately of Shaw, Benny Goodman, Tommy Dorsey, Jimmy Dorsey, Harry James, Glenn Miller, Count Basie, Duke Ellington. Let me dwell for a moment on just three of these remarkable fellows.

Start with Harry James of the handsome looks and the two first names. The trumpeter, who earned his stripes on Benny Goodman's bandstand before setting up shop for himself married the pinup girl with the million-dollar legs whom GIs on both fronts yearned for during World War II. Betty Grable mentions her bandleader husband enthusiastically in *How to Marry a Millionaire*, an in-joke in the spirit of Lauren Bacall (Mrs. Humphrey Bogart) when she refers in the same movie to "the old guy" in *The African Queen*. Listen to James's rendering of "You Made Me Love You." I think of it as virtually a translation of Judy Garland's vocal (from her "Dear Mr. Gable" days) into the language of a trumpet solo. The lanky bandleader also appeared as himself in movies.

Then there's Artie Shaw—that is, Abraham Arthur Arshawsky. Artie Shaw excelled at all he did. He was a legitimate intellectual but also a crack marksman, a skillful fly fisherman, and an ornery cuss who could simply walk away from a triumphant gig, disband his group, go to Mexico, return with "Frenesí," vow never to play again, quit, and feel nothing but disdain for the public, his fans included. Artie's *amour-propre* may help explain his appeal to the ladies. He was married eight times—to Lana Turner, Ava Gardner, and Jerome Kern's daughter, Betty, among others. On his honeymoon with Gardner, he brought along Darwin's *On the Origin of Species*, which makes a certain kind of intellectual sense when you think about it, but is not the usual fare of lovers on a spree. Darwin's great-grandson deemed Ava to be "the highest specimen of the human species." But Artie thought she was a dummy, and she was desperately in love with Artie. "I don't think he ever really understood the damage he did," Ava said about Artie Shaw. When the conversation touched on serious matters, he would tell her she wasn't entitled to an opinion because she had not read Dostoyevsky, Thomas Mann, and Flaubert, not to mention Schopenhauer and Nietzsche. Well, as Sammy Cahn observed, if Frank had treated her the way Artie Shaw did, he might have held her.

Some connoisseurs prefer Shaw's clarinet even to Goodman's, but bespectacled Benny was the public face of swing from the time of his Carnegie Hall concert in 1938. The Goodman band made exceptional music and featured exceptional personnel (the arranger Fletcher Henderson; the singers Peggy Lee, Martha Tilton, and Helen Ward; the drummer Gene Krupa; et al.) The self-absorbed clarinetist was, in Helen Forrest's judgment, "by far the most unpleasant person I ever met in music."*

---

*A man I know gave the aging Benny a tour of Baltimore. When he pointed out the place where Edgar Allan Poe is buried, Benny said: "What was his instrument?"

I believe it. After his death, Benny's musicians started a joke: The good news is, the great bandleader has died. The bad news is, he didn't suffer. Even so, no one caught the sound, the drive, and the tempo of the era better than the Goodman band playing "Sing, Sing, Sing."

After Sinatra, the position of bandleader was never again what it had been—a symbol of male glamour on a par with home run–hitting centerfielders, astronauts, and Hollywood stars.

11

IN THE 1940S, if you asked the men of the armed services, Crosby would come out on top. If you asked the women who stayed back home, it was Sinatra all the way. Groaner versus crooner, establishment versus upstart, "White Christmas" versus "Saturday Night Is the Loneliest Night in the Week."

Bing Crosby was the gold standard of American popular singers, almost from the time he joined the Paul Whiteman Orchestra in 1926. Crosby was Sinatra's original inspiration. Early on, before he and Nancy Barbato were married, they caught Crosby's act at the Loew's Journal Square Theater in Jersey City in 1933. "He's a troubadour," Frank said excitedly. "He tells a story in every song. He's relaxed, but he makes you feel like he's singing just for you." Sinatra told Nancy he bet he could sing like that. He was seventeen.

When Sinatra was Dorsey's boy singer, he approached the editor of *Metronome* and lobbied to be put on the cover. "There's only Crosby and me, and he won't be around forever," Sinatra said.

The competitive streak was always strong in Sinatra. E. J. Kahn in his 1946 *New Yorker* profile of Sinatra acknowledged the professional discretion behind his reluctance to slam the competitor's product, but noted that such inhibitions fell away if a rival's name caught him off guard—"I can sing that son of a bitch off the stage any day of the week!"

In public, of course, humility was called for, and the wise

move was always to depict Bing and Frank as respectful rivals, even show-biz buds, rather than as competitors for the distinction of being the nation's favorite voice. On the air in November 1944 the two sang a "parody medley" in which the lyrics of popular tunes were adapted to suit the competition between this "chummy pair." The audience's delight comes from recognizing a familiar melody put to new comic use. Crosby got the best lines. About the advent of "Frankie boy": "*oy vay* this should happen to me," to the tune of "It Could Happen to You." To the tune of "I'll Get By," Crosby quips that he got by all right "until they heard from you." The kid from Hoboken gets to be courtly: "There's just one Bing / Long live the king," leaving Bing to wonder: "How can that voice come from 'Out of Nowhere'?"

Friendly rivals: Frank and Bing.

Silver Screen Collection / Getty Images

12

THE BATTLE OF the baritones raged in the 1940s. If I were
a disc jockey I would begin an hour by playing Jack Leonard
("In the Still of the Night"), then Perry Como ("Mountain
Greenery"), Bob Eberly ("Brazil"), and Dick Haymes ("It
Might As Well Be Spring"), saving Sinatra for last ("Imagina-
tion"). After a break I'd play something by Crosby, the reigning champ, though I'd probably pick a Crosby recording of
the previous decade, "Pennies from Heaven" or "Brother, Can
You Spare a Dime?" I think I'd also play a song called "Dick
Haymes, Dick Todd, and Como," in which Sinatra sang about
three of his rivals who were "breathin' on my neck." A parody
of the now-forgotten hit tune "Sunday, Monday, and Always,"
it had lyrics specially written by Sammy Cahn to suit the predicament of a singer confronted with competition. When, in the
middle of the song, Sinatra substitutes "Perry" for "Como" and
in a spoken aside says, "That's the other guy's first name," you
grasp in an instant the difference between *Sinatra the voice* and
Sinatra the mouth. When he sang, the voice was that of an angel,
exquisite in enunciation, pure of tone. But the mouth always
had a lot of Hoboken in it, and you hear it when he talks. The
song ends with the affirmation that there's "just one Crosby,"
but there's room enough for all the rest.

Late in life, Crosby was asked to name his favorite scene
from all the movies he had made. He had partnered with Fred
Astaire, Bob Hope, Louis Armstrong, Danny Kaye, Rosemary

Clooney, Dorothy Lamour, Judy Garland, and the Andrews Sisters. But his favorite was "Well, Did You Evah?" the duet he sings with Sinatra and a glass of the bubbly in the Cole Porter musical *High Society*.

Bing got used to being compared to the younger man. Frank "is a singer who comes along once in a lifetime," Crosby quipped, "but why did he have to come in mine?"

HERE'S A QUICK test. Match the Italian-American singer
with his real name. I am including Harry Warren, the great
Italian-American songwriter who composed the music for
"You'll Never Know," "I Had the Craziest Dream," "That's
Amore," "Jeepers Creepers," "Chattanooga Choo Choo,"
"There Will Never be Another You," and "You're Getting to
Be a Habit with Me":

Vic Damone	Gennaro Luigi Vitaliano
Perry Como	Antonio Benedetto
Connie Francis	Francesco Steven Castellucio
Tony Bennett	Vito Rocco Farinola
Dean Martin	Salvatore Guargna
Bobby Darin	Dino Paul Crocetti
Harry Warren	Pierino Ronald Coma
Frankie Laine	Roberto Cassotto
Jerry Vale	Concetta Rosemarie Franconero
Frankie Valli	Francesco Paolo LoVecchio
Frank Sinatra	Francis Albert Sinatra

STUDY THE MUSICAL career of Frank Sinatra—his work with the James and Dorsey bands, and with arrangers as skillful as Don Costa, Neal Hefti, Gordon Jenkins, Quincy Jones, Johnny Mandel, Billy May, Sy Oliver, Nelson Riddle, George Siravo, and Axel Stordahl—and you reach the inescapable conclusion that the enterprise of songwriting, like that of moviemaking, is intrinsically collaborative, and that this may be a ground condition for any popular art in a technologically savvy modern, or postmodern, era. When it comes to classic American popular songs, the model of creation involves a division of labor among specialists: composer, lyricist, and arranger on one side, singer and musicians on the other, with the line between "creative" and "interpretive" artists increasingly blurred. When all the specialists involved are possessed of genius—when Rodgers wrote the tune and Hart wrote the lyric and Riddle has done the charts and Sinatra is the singer and the instrumentalists are Hollywood's best—you get "The Lady Is a Tramp," and this is as it should be.

COCKY, HE WAS always that. When Sinatra was a twenty-three-year-old nobody who lucked into a gig with Harry James's band, the bandleader was asked about his new boy singer. "Not so loud," James said. "He considers himself the greatest vocalist in the business. Get that! Nobody ever heard of him. He's never had a hit record. He looks like a wet mop. But he says he's the greatest. If he hears you compliment him, he'll demand a raise tonight."

Fearless, too. Although he couldn't read music, he did not let that incidental handicap stop him. He contributed lyrics to songs. He heard a new song once or twice and knew it cold.* He was even known to wield a baton. In 1946, Sinatra conducted *Frank Sinatra Conducts the Music of Alec Wilder*, an excellent album of thirteen Wilder compositions, including works for oboe, bassoon, and flute. Sinatra handled the woodwinds deftly. Ten years later, the first album recorded in the landmark Capitol Records Tower in Los Angeles—the thirteen-story building

---

*"I don't read a note of music. I learn songs by having them played for me a couple of times while I read the lyrics. I can pick up the melody very quickly. I learn the lyrics by writing them out in long hand. When I get a new song, I look for continuity of melody that in itself will tell a musical story. It must go somewhere. I don't like it to ramble. And then, by the same token, I like almost the same thing—more, as a matter of fact—in the lyrics. They must tell you a complete story, from 'once upon a time' to 'the end.'" Ben Cosgrove, "The Private World and Thoughts of Frank Sinatra," *Life*, April 23, 1965.

that resembles a stack of records—was *Frank Sinatra Conducts Tone Poems of Color.* The composers of the "tone poems" were some of Hollywood's top arrangers: Victor Young, Gordon Jenkins, Billy May, Nelson Riddle, Alec Wilder, Elmer Bernstein, Jeff Alexander, and André Previn.

16

SUMMERTIME, BUT THE livin' ain't easy. It is 1939 and the news is bad. Europe is headed toward war. Everyone knows it and almost everyone dreads it. The final straw is the nonaggression pact negotiated by the foreign ministers of Nazi Germany and Soviet Russia, von Ribbentrop and Molotov. Signed in August, the agreement gives Hitler a free hand to roll his tanks into the countries on either side of Germany: first Poland to the east, then France and Belgium and Holland to the west. Hitler has taken Austria, the Rhineland, and Czechoslovakia without resistance. His next move will trigger the cataclysm. Stalin, meanwhile, will gobble up Finland. Churchill can see it happening. So can Roosevelt, to whom the threat is not nearly so immediate. It is just a matter of time.

In music, the big bands are playing, and the joint is jumpin'. When the decade is young, the Duke Ellington Orchestra and the voice of Ivie Anderson deliver the message: "It don't mean a thing if it ain't got that swing." In Hollywood, Jerome Kern and Dorothy Fields collaborate on songs for Fred Astaire and Ginger Rogers to sing and dance to in *Swing Time*. "The Way You Look Tonight," which Fred sings to Ginger, walks off with the year's Academy Award for best song in 1936. Swing officially becomes king in 1938 when the Benny Goodman Orchestra gives a concert in Carnegie Hall that is hailed as a breakthrough. Goodman starts with Berlin's "Blue Skies," Gershwin's "I Got Rhythm," and Rodgers's "Blue Room" and moves on to "Stompin' at the Savoy" and "Sing, Sing, Sing," the very sound of the decade with Gene Krupa on the drums.

In 1939 the most successful bands in the country were those of Goodman, Artie Shaw, Tommy Dorsey, and Glenn Miller. The top singers were Bing Crosby, Jack Leonard, and Bob Eberly on the male side and Ella Fitzgerald, Mildred Bailey, and Billie Holiday among the women. The Benny Goodman band's recording of "And the Angels Sing," Ziggy Elman's klezmer classic with lyrics by Johnny Mercer, was the top song. The previous year's biggest hit, Artie Shaw's "Begin the Beguine," was still up there, and Glenn Miller had three hits on his hands: "Moonlight Serenade," "In the Mood," and "Little Brown Jug." Harry James's "Ciribiribin" made it into the top ten and became his theme song.

On Thursday, August 31, 1939, Frank Sinatra and the Harry James Orchestra recorded "All or Nothing at All" (music, Arthur Altman; words, Jack Lawrence). The boy singer stretched his two-octive range to the max by hitting a high F at the end of the song. It sold eight thousand copies when originally released and a million when rereleased four years later. Two things had happened in the interim. James Caesar Petrillo, the despotic head of the American Federation of Musicians, called for a strike of instrumentalists to commence on August 1, 1942. Columbia Records was desperate for material other than that produced by a lonely voice surrounded by a syrupy a cappella chorus in place of musical instruments. The second thing that had happened was the phenomenon. Call it what you will: Frankophilia, Swoonatra, the rise of the unlikely bony heartthrob with the big Adam's apple, the "Voice That Has Thrilled Millions."

On Thursday, August 31, 1939, Germany issued an ultimatum, making sixteen demands of Poland and its allies, none of them realistic, and Britain began evacuating children and invalids from London to country shires. The next day Germany marched into Poland, firing the first shots of a conflict destined to end in the unconditional surrender of one side or the other. The ambiguities that marked the end of World War I would stand as a lesson to President Roosevelt. This time there would be no negotiated outcome. This time it would be all or nothing at all.

17

HARRY JAMES'S TRUMPET is less prominent on "All or Nothing at All" than in such tunes as "You Made Me Love You" and "I've Heard That Song Before," two songs Woody Allen loves to use in his films. "All or Nothing at All" is not brassy, exclamatory, breezy, assertive. The singer's voice is paramount, and Sinatra here, comfortable even when he elevates into tenor range, softens his voice to an intimate tenderness. The lyrics have him falling uncontrollably in love—and imagining the tidal consequences "if I fell / under the spell" of the siren's call. He would be lost, vanquished by waves of passion, caught in the undertow. From this position of weakness, the lyrics draw strength. Because of his vulnerability, the singer demands absolute love, unconditionally bestowed. No compromises. The last notes of the song coincide with the repetition of the title phrase. And suddenly, on the last word, "all," the singer reaches for the highest note available to him and sustains it improbably, climactically.

Jack Lawrence wrote a fine lyric for "All or Nothing at All." The rhyme of "appealed to me" and "could yield to me" is first class. The title alone beguiles with its symmetry: "nothing" sandwiched between two iterations of "all." But what distinguishes the recording is how the young singer, a season shy of his twenty-fourth birthday, has caught and embodied the spirit of the words; how well he communicates that quality of vulnerability mixed with intransigence; his insistence on the genuine ("if it's real") and his refusal to settle for half measures. Not to mention the clarity of his diction—each word clear, precise, exact.

"All or Nothing at All" launched the pattern. It is the first time a Sinatra song seems to have an autobiographical or allegorical dimension—a resonance that seems undeniable in retrospect, and may have been obvious even at the time. It is also a glimpse into a character that would come to represent the American male as a type. The character manages at once to be lonely and somehow pitiable, a little guy dwarfed physically by others but making up for it with a confidence that the singer's sustained last note conveys. And he is an absolutist—he wants all, not some, and will show a marked predilection for "all" songs: "All the Things You Are," "It All Depends on You," "All of Me," "All the Way," "All I Need Is the Girl." There's a couplet in the Gus Kahn standard "Love Me or Leave Me" that applies to Sinatra in love: love is not something he wants to "borrow," to enjoy for a day but to "give back tomorrow."

Martin Scorsese pays careful attention to his soundtracks. Listen closely and you will hear Sinatra sing "All or Nothing at All" on the portable radios at poolside when Jake LaMotta (Robert De Niro) first sets his eyes on the luscious blond babe in sunglasses and two-piece, the love of his life, Vikki (Cathy Moriarty), whom he will marry, in *Raging Bull*.

18

BY THE END of 1939, Sinatra was recruited by Tommy Dorsey, "the sentimental gentleman of swing," who was not necessarily a gentleman but was an exemplary bandleader, demanding and uncompromising. An outstanding soloist on trombone, he recruited such talents as those of trumpeters Bunny Berigan and Ziggy Elman; pianist and songwriter Joe Bushkin; arranger and songwriter Sy Oliver; drummer Buddy Rich; vocalists Jo Stafford, Connie Haines, and Edythe Wright. One of Dorsey's arrangers, trumpeter Axel Stordahl, achieved greater fame when he left the band to serve as Sinatra's arranger. A third trombonist hired in the late 1940s, Nelson Riddle, turned out to be the most celebrated of all Sinatra's arrangers.

Dorsey heard Sinatra on the radio and hired him away from James for his own vastly more successful band. He raised Sinatra's salary to $125 a week. Sinatra would replace Jack Leonard, a fine crooner ("Marie," "In the Still of the Night"), who had left the Dorsey band to strike out on his own.

Sinatra hated leaving the James band. The last night was in Buffalo, in January 1940, and Sinatra never forgot it. "The bus pulled out with the rest of the guys after midnight. I'd said goodbye to them all, and it was snowing. I remember there was nobody around, and I stood alone with my suitcase in the snow and watched the taillights of the bus disappear. Then the tears started, and I tried to run after the bus."

When Sinatra joined Tommy, Jo Stafford, a member of the

Pied Pipers, the band's vocal group, remembers how thin he looked, "almost fragile looking. When he stepped up to the microphone, we all smirked and looked at each other, waiting to see what he could do. The first song he did was 'Stardust.' I know it sounds like something out of a B movie, but it's true: Before he'd sung four bars, we knew. We knew he was going to be a great star."

19

WITH THE DORSEY band Sinatra sang "I'll Never Smile Again," "Polka Dots and Moonbeams," "How About You?," "I'll Be Seeing You," "Without a Song," "Everything Happens to Me," "There Are Such Things," "The One I Love Belongs to Somebody Else," "East of the Sun," "Oh! Look at Me Now," "Frenesí." If you were to play one tune from the Dorsey period that could stand as a model for an imaginative big band vocal arrangement, you might choose the jubilant escape song "Let's Get Away from It All," in which the protagonists plan to visit all the forty-eight states of the union. Connie Haines: "I'll get a new Southern drawl." Sinatra: "Another one?" The Pied Pipers get to joke about a second visit to Niagara, which was shorthand for honeymoon and was therefore a socially acceptable way to talk about having sex— "This time we're digging the falls."

From the start, Sinatra worked to improve his technique. Harry James encouraged him to learn to jump rope, to gain strength and lung capacity. But it was from Dorsey's mastery of the trombone that Sinatra learned a critical lesson in breath control: how to stretch a note, or link the last note of one phrase with the first note of the next, without pausing for breath. Sinatra worked hard at it. He swam for hours in swimming pools, with long stretches underwater, to develop this capacity.

You'll hear Sinatra sing past a stanza break—or negotiate the transition from bridge to chorus seamlessly—in "Without a Song," where he glides from the end of the bridge ("in my soul!") through the beginning of the final chorus ("I'll never know"). You'll hear something similarly breathtaking in "April in Paris." In "My Funny Valentine," his voice closes the gap between the penultimate line ("Stay, little valentine, stay!") and the final phrase ("Each day is Valentine's Day"). Similar feats of vocal artistry are to be found also in the early "Fools Rush In" and "Put Your Dreams Away" and, decades later, in a late live performance of "The Shadow of Your Smile." Sinatra can hold a note for longer than seems humanly possible before moving into the next musical phrase.

I have always thought of this trick of his as a musical equivalent of the way the *liaison* works in French pronunciation—where the end of one word melts or slides into the beginning of the next one. The gap between the words, or notes, is eliminated. The voice dominates the silence. It's as if there were a foot pedal to extend the life of the sound. On the radio I just heard him do "Don't Worry 'Bout Me" at a late concert. His voice could no longer do certain things, but he still managed the liaison between the title phrase and "I'll get along." Most singers would pause to breathe. It is the natural thing to do. Not Sinatra.

Nor is this mere virtuosity. The point of the gesture is to convey depth of emotion.

A comparison to Marlon Brando is in order. "As a singer Sinatra prided himself on his clear diction, yet it could be said that he developed close musical equivalents of the Brando mumble," the literary scholar Roger Gilbert writes. "His

slurring portamentos and glissandos, his tendency to stay
behind the beat, his willingness to let hints of raspiness enter his
voice, his sudden shifts of dynamic and timbre, all these become
part of an expressive vocabulary that does with musical notes
what a Method actor does with words."*

*Roger Gilbert, "Singing in the Moment: Sinatra and the Culture of the
Fifties," in *Sinatra: The Man, The Music, The Legend*, eds. Jeanne Fuchs
and Ruth Prigozy (University of Rochester Press, 2007), p. 57.

20

"DORSEY WAS THE greatest melodic trombonist in the business, but he was a drag to work for," Buddy Rich said, understating the case. TD's theme song was "I'm Getting Sentimental over You." And there is a quality to his playing, perhaps especially when he mutes his horn, which for want of a better word one might call sentimental, sweet, or soulful. But he was anything but sentimental in matters of money. When Sinatra decided to go out on his own, Dorsey forced him to sign a punitive contract that would grant Dorsey a percentage of all the singer's future royalties. Sinatra thought it worth the risk. Later he managed to slip out of the contract altogether, though it cost him plenty. "I hope you fall on your ass," Dorsey told the singer. Dorsey wanted Sinatra to fail, and Sinatra never fully forgave him, though he did turn up unannounced to toast the bandleader and sing at a memorable Dorsey tribute in New York in February 1955. (If you can find the CD called *This One's for Tommy*, featuring Sinatra and Jo Stafford, buy it.) One of the first albums Sinatra did with the Reprise label was *I Remember Tommy* in 1961, with arrangements by Sy Oliver. A treat: play the 1961 versions of "East of the Sun (and West of the Moon)" and "The One I Love Belongs to Somebody Else" back to back with recordings the old Dorsey band made twenty years earlier.

Years later—in Los Angeles, in June 1979—Sinatra introduced Harry James to a live audience. James was a great guy. James had let him out of his contract after only six months.

"And then there was Tommy Dorsey," Sinatra said. "And when I wanted to get out of my contract to him years later, it cost me seven million dollars." Suddenly the specter of Tommy Dorsey materialized before him as a ghost before a Shakespearean prince. "You hear me, Tommy? You hear me? I'm talking to you."

21

IN *THE GODFATHER*, Michael Corleone (Al Pacino) explains to his girlfriend Kay Adams (Diane Keaton) how his father had liberated the famous singer Johnny Fontane (Al Martino) from the punitive "personal services" contract a bandleader had made him sign as a precondition to allowing him to leave the band. "My father made him an offer he couldn't refuse," Michael says. "Luca Brazzi held a gun to his forehead, and my father assured him that either his brains or his signature would be on this sheet of paper."

The Dorsey contract would have obliged Sinatra to pay Dorsey one third of all future earnings beyond a hundred bucks a week for the next ten years. An additional ten percent was earmarked for the bandleader's manager. The tactic is not unheard of in corporate America, where it is commonly known as a "poison-pill clause," designed to protect a company from being acquired by a larger company or corporate raider.

What really happened to liberate Sinatra from his Dorsey obligation? The cover story is that going solo cost Sinatra and his backers some $60,000—a considerable sum in the 1940s, but a fraction of the amount that Dorsey would have garnered if he hadn't listened to reason in the persons of three fellows, one of whom was said to be mobster Willie Moretti. According to Dorsey's own account, "Willie fingered a gun and told me he was glad to hear that I was letting Frank out of our deal. I took the hint." The lawyers did the rest.

One irony is that the contract was never valid in the first place, because Harry James let Sinatra out of their contract with a simple handshake and never got around to tearing up the piece of legal paper. ("The word is stronger than the pen with me," James said.) But none of the players knew that in 1942 and '43.

22

ON DECEMBER 30, 1942, at the Paramount Theater in Times Square, the Benny Goodman band was the main attraction. When Goodman took a break, comedian Jack Benny, doing somebody a favor, introduced the next act—a kid he didn't even know. What followed the mention of Frank Sinatra's name was a deafening roar. "Five thousand kids, stamping, yelling, screaming, applauding. I was scared stiff. I couldn't move a muscle," Sinatra said later.

When the roar went up, Goodman turned around and snapped: "What the fuck was that?"

What it was, was a brand-new phenomenon.

Frank was the first boy singer to trigger mass teenage female hysteria—more than a decade before Elvis, and a score of years before the Beatles—and it is worth noting that Swoonatra's bobby-soxers had the good sense to time their cries of rapture in such a way that you could still hear the words of the songs.

In John O'Hara's story "The Father," from his 1962 collection *The Cape Cod Lighter*, the forty-two-year-old husband in a long-term marriage that long ago turned dreary receives a letter from his sister with a tabloid news clipping from 1943, when he was overseas. The clip includes a photo of his future wife, seventeen-year-old Vilma Schrock, with three other girls from Trenton, New Jersey. The girls were "huddled behind a sign" that read "Frankie Boy Is the Most—The Sinatra Swooners, Trenton N.J." According to the caption, the girls had been waiting outside the Paramount since seven in the morning, "and at the time the picture was taken they had been waiting four hours and probably would have to wait four more, because the kids who were already in the theater were refusing to leave when the show was over." Nothing else happens, but when the story ends, the husband has tears in his eyes, not only for his wife and teenage daughter but for himself.

A Sinatra engagement at the Paramount caused the Columbus Day riots of 1944. He did nine shows a day in those days, starting at 8:10 a.m. and winding down at 2:30 the next morning. During an average day he might sing one hundred songs. The theater could seat well over three thousand, and if you played hooky from school and managed to snag one of those seats, you didn't give it up. You brought peanut-butter sandwiches in a paper bag to sustain you. After some shows, as few as 250 spectators left the theater.

Why did the bobby-soxers shriek and moan and go crazy and wet their pants rather than vacate the Paramount, and other such theaters, in 1942 and 1944? What caused such a widespread abandonment of female modesty and dignity?

It was rumored that press agents encouraged the hysteria, but that's not really what happened. The press agents—and Sinatra had great ones—may have worked their butts off, but the girls needed little inducement to let themselves go.

In a *Cosmopolitan* article from 1956, Adela Rogers St. John described the tumult of a Sinatra appearance in the early 1940s where "hordes of raving bobby-soxers attempted to tear off his clothes whenever he showed his emaciated face and angular figure."

Keith Richards of the Rolling Stones encountered something similar twenty years later. "The power of the teenage females of thirteen, fourteen, fifteen, when they're in a gang, has never left me," he wrote in his memoir *Life*. "They nearly killed me. I was never more in fear for my life than I was from teenage girls. The ones that choked me, tore me to shreds, if you got caught in a frenzied crowd of them—it's hard to express how frightening they could be. You'd rather be in a trench fighting the enemy than to be faced with this unstoppable, killer wave of lust and desire, or whatever it is—it's unknown even to them. The cops are running away, and you're faced with this savagery of unleashed emotions."

The poet Carolyn Kizer, who was eighteen when Sinatra burst on the scene, reasons that the bobby-soxers of the 1940s lost their hearts to young Frankie because he was androgynous, combining masculine and feminine traits, that big voice coming out of that undernourished body. Was it a matter of maternal instincts kicking in? "Not really," she replies. "You see, he seemed able to express regret without self-pity, vulnerability with no loss of masculinity." I thought that was an excellent answer, better than the theory that he was a substitute for the lads overseas—which would leave you with the question: Why Sinatra? Why not Dick Haymes?

When the unretired Frank did his Main Event concert at Madison Square Garden on October 13, 1974, Martha Weinman Lear wrote a review appearing under the headline "The Bobby Sox Have Wilted, but the Memory Remains Fresh." "What could have driven me so crazy?" she wonders, recollecting the days she spent as a young teen swooning through four shows at the RKO-Boston. " 'Frankie!' we screamed from the balcony, because you couldn't get an orchestra seat unless you were standing on line at dawn, and how could you explain to Mom leaving for school before dawn? 'Frankie, I *love you*!' And that glorious shouldered spaghetti strand way down there in the spotlight would croon on serenely, giving us a quick little flick of a smile or, as a special bonus, a sidelong tremor of the lower lip. I used to bring binoculars just to watch that lower lip. And then, the other thing. The voice had that *trick,* you know, that funny little sliding, skimming slur that it would do coming off the end of a note."

Even the most starstruck bobby-soxer registered that Sinatra glissando. On a gig in Dallas, back when he was singing with Dorsey, the bandleader noticed that girls sighed when he did that, and he instructed the musicians to put down their instruments and sigh in unison when it happened. According to the *Saturday Evening Post,* in 1946, "that is the sole basis for the legend that the sighing and swooning over Sinatra was started and shrewdly fostered by smart press agents. Sinatra had no press agent until after he was a star." Even after Dorsey called off the gag, the girls continued to shriek and sigh. And the boys wondered where they could get the funny-shaped bow ties he wore.

Lear confides that she and her equally demented friends used to "practice swooning" before they went to hear Sinatra sing. Later, as they grew up, a lot of things changed. But "I tell you, the gravity was as powerful as ever" when, by then married to the producer of *Come Blow Your Horn* (1963), she met Frank at the movie's opening-night party. All at once was she "a child again, beguiled again, zooming backward through time and space, shaking like a thirteen-year-old." And now, now, "the blue eyes still burn," and "what's left of the voice still gets to me like no other voice, and it always will."

The Main Event at Madison Square Garden, which occasioned Lear's reminiscence, is not my favorite Sinatra concert. But it does have one amazing feature: The singer is introduced by Howard Cosell at his most magniloquent: "Live from New York . . . a city that pulsates always . . . and in the heart of the metropolis the great arena, Madison Square Garden, which has created and housed so many champions . . . the most enduring champion of them all, Frank Sinatra, comes to the entire Western Hemisphere live with the Main Event: Frank Sinatra in concert." In the background the strings play "It Was a Very Good Year," and then they switch to "All the Way," and Cosell goes on, ad-libbing majestically, with the breathless excitement worthy of a heavyweight championship fight.

23

WHEN SINATRA MET Humphrey Bogart, the star of *Casablanca* and *The Maltese Falcon* said that he'd heard Sinatra knew how to make women faint. "Make me faint," Bogart said.

Sinatra joined Bogart and such other Hollywood stars as Bette Davis, Rita Hayworth, Orson Welles, Danny Kaye, and Edward G. Robinson on the FDR bandwagon in 1944.

On September 28, 1944, Sinatra enjoyed an audience with President Roosevelt in the White House. The singer, who was in favor of an unprecedented fourth term for FDR, had wangled an invitation when the Democratic Committee chairman asked restaurateur Toots Shor to a reception at the White House. FDR was glad to have him; it would counteract Bing Crosby's endorsement of his opponent, Republican Thomas E. Dewey, governor of New York, Roosevelt's old job before he went to the White House. "Look who's here," Roosevelt exclaimed and asked the singer to confide in him the title of the song that would be number one on the hit parade next week. "I won't tell." FDR grinned. "Amapola," Sinatra said. (The title may have sounded Italian to the president—and Italy was an uncomfortable subject in wartime—so he switched the subject.)* The meeting went well,

---

*Possibly the Jimmy Dorsey version, with vocals by Bob Eberly and Helen O'Connell. "Amapola (Pretty Little Poppy)" was Jimmy Dorsey's biggest hit, occupying the top rung for ten weeks in 1941. You'll hear the song used hauntingly on the soundtrack of the great Sergio Leone movie *Once Upon*

though the president was said afterward to scratch his head in wonderment at the idea that the skinny crooner had mastered the art of making girls faint. "He would never have made them swoon in our day," he told an aide after the party broke up.

Sinatra donated money to FDR's campaign, made radio broadcasts, spoke at Carnegie Hall. "I'd just like to tell you what a great guy Roosevelt is," he said. "I was a little stunned when I stood alongside him. I thought, here's the greatest guy alive today and here's a little guy from Hoboken shaking his hand. He knows about everything—even my racket." Conservative columnists predictably had a field day with Sinatra's self-importance. At a concert Sinatra sang a parody lyric of "Everything Happens to Me." The Republicans were "mad as they can be," because he went to Washington to have a cup of tea with "a man called Franklin D."

FDR, of course, hovered over the popular culture of the time like a benevolent deity. Of the many movies and songs in which FDR is a vital presence, there are two I like best. In *Yankee Doodle Dandy*, the action begins and ends in the Oval Office, where James Cagney as George M. Cohan has gone to receive a commendation from the commander in chief. You never see FDR but you hear an approximation of his voice, and the expression on Cagney's face tells you all you need to know about the president's authority. In *Babes on Broadway* (1941), Judy Garland and Mickey Rooney sing "How About You?" (music, Burton Lane; lyrics, Ralph Freed), a song also covered

---

a Time in America. In October 1944, however, the number-one songs as charted by *Billboard* were Dinah Shore's cover of "I'll Walk Alone" and the Mills Brothers with "You Always Hurt the One You Love."

by Tommy Dorsey's best boy singer. There's a moment in the song when the vocalist—who likes New York in June, Gershwin tunes, potato chips, moonlight, good books, and holding hands in the movies—tells us that "Franklin Roosevelt's looks give me a thrill."*

*Recording the tune for the *Songs for Swingin' Lovers* album in 1956, Sinatra substitutes "James Durante's looks."

24

SOMETIMES OVERSHADOWED BY the Capitol Years, from 1953 to 1961, or the years after, when "our hoodlum singer" (as Johnny Carson put it at a St. Louis Rat Pack concert) founded his own record company, the 1940s are the closest thing to an overlooked decade in Frank Sinatra's career. The songs Sinatra sang in the forties—whether with the James or Dorsey bands or on his own records for the Columbia label—could provide most of the soundtrack for any documentary of that decade. This is a lovely way to spend an evening.

1.

"All or Nothing at All" (music, Arthur Altman; lyrics, Jack Lawrence). Though initially recorded in 1939, this most famous of the songs Sinatra sang with the Harry James Orchestra is included here on a technicality. The 1939 recording didn't become a hit until it was rereleased as a single four years later. Sinatra in 1944: "It's a funny thing about that song. The recording we made of it five years ago is now in one of the top spots among the best sellers. But it's the same old recording. It's also the song I used to audition for Tommy Dorsey, who signed me on the strength of it. And now it's my first big record."

2.

"I'll Never Smile Again" (Ruth Lowe). As recorded on May 23, 1940, by the Dorsey orchestra with Sinatra and the Pied Pipers

In the studio for Columbia.

Michael Ochs Archives / Getty Images

vocal group. A breakout hit. One of the Dorsey songs Sinatra will record as a solo in his Capitol period, with a Gordon Jenkins arrangement, on *No One Cares*.

3.

"Oh! Look at Me Now" (music, Joe Bushkin; lyrics, John De Vries). January 6, 1941. Another landmark from the three years Sinatra spent as Tommy Dorsey's boy singer. Sung as a duet with Connie Haines backed by the Pied Pipers. In the allegory of Sinatra's career, this song—which he rerecorded as a solo arranged by Nelson Riddle on *A Swingin' Affair* in 1957—figures heavily: "I'm so proud I'm bustin' my vest."

4.

"Be Careful, It's My Heart" (words and music, Irving Berlin). June 9, 1942. Like Artie Shaw, Sinatra recognized the value of recording a repertory of songs written by the masters, and thus he did as much as anyone to (*a*) extend the life of the music, and (*b*) launch the concept of "the standard." In this excellent Dorsey arrangement of an underrated Berlin ballad, Tommy's trombone sweetly states the melody all the way, and then Sinatra's vocal follows suit.

5.

"(There'll Be a) Hot Time in the Town of Berlin" (music, Joe Bushkin; lyrics, John De Vries). I've heard two versions of this tune, which Bushkin, singer Lee Wiley's pianist, wrote to boost morale among our troops abroad. The CBS radio broadcast of October 17, 1943, which became a V-disc, is swell, but I prefer the more relaxed delivery of March 4, 1944 (arranged by Axel Stordahl, and available on the box set *Frank Sinatra in*

Hollywood).* This is one of "the songs that fought the war," in theater critic John Bush Jones's phrase. Our lads were going on "to take a hike / through Hitler's Reich" and amend his "Heil" to "whatcha-know-Joe" or "gimme some skin."

6.

"Dick Haymes, Dick Todd, and Como." October 23, 1944. Sammy Cahn, who could craft a lyric at a moment's notice, took "Sunday, Monday, and Always," the Johnny Burke and Jimmy Van Heusen hit, and substituted these lyrics about some of the competitors in the battle of the baritones. You'll find it on Columbia's *The V-Discs* box. There are jokes about the singer's lack of heft and the bobby-soxers' adoring screams, which yet may cause him grief, "but if they ever stop / I'll find that I'm back on relief."

7.

"All the Things You Are" (music, Jerome Kern; lyrics, Oscar Hammerstein II). Recorded January 29, 1945. Axel Stordahl and orchestra. The apotheosis of the great American love song, from one of Broadway's two greatest melodists. Concluding crescendo illustrates young singer's high range. From *The Best of the Columbia Years, 1943–1952.*

8.

"Where or When" (music, Richard Rodgers; lyrics, Lorenz Hart). See comment (above) on "All the Things You Are," recorded on the same day.

---

*V-Discs—the "V" for Victory—were released for soldiers and sailors serving overseas during World War II.

9.

"Saturday Night (Is the Loneliest Night in the Week)" (music, Jule Styne; lyrics, Sammy Cahn). Recorded on February 3, 1945, "Saturday Night" is an instant metonymy for the home front during World War II.

10.

"Put Your Dreams Away" (Ruth Lowe, Paul Mann, Stephen Weiss). Recorded May 1, 1945. Sinatra's radio—and later his TV—theme music. A full-throated display of his ability to sustain a note seemingly past the breaking point.

11.

"Oh Bess, Oh Where's My Bess?" (George Gershwin, DuBose Heyward, Ira Gershwin). Recorded February 24, 1946. When Sinatra worked the Wedgwood Room at the Waldorf in late November 1945, he opened with "Paper Moon," sang "Laura" and "It Might as Well Be Spring," and surprised the critics most with this selection from *Porgy and Bess*. The singer's emotional identification with his material reaches operatic heights.

12.

"That Old Black Magic" (music, Harold Arlen; lyrics, Johnny Mercer). Recorded March 10, 1946. Arlen, the jazziest of the songwriters, and according to Ethel Waters, the "Negro-est" white man she knew, wrote songs of extraordinary complexity. In Mercer he found his ideal lyricist: "For you're the lover I have waited for / The mate that fate had me created for."

13.

"The Coffee Song (They've Got an Awful Lot of Coffee in Brazil)." The music is by Dick Miles, the lyrics by Bob Hilliard, the same fellow who wrote "In the Wee Small Hours of the Morning." Recorded July 24, 1946. A charming nightclub number reflecting the late 1940s fascination with South America. In Brazil, folks use "coffee ketchup" to spice their ham and eggs, and "coffee pickles way outsell the dill." Close your eyes and you're at the Copa.

14.

"Begin the Beguine" (Cole Porter). October 19, 1946. Arranged by George Siravo, who was responsible for Sinatra's best charts until Nelson Riddle at Capitol. Porter liked to say that the key to writing Broadway hits was to "write Jewish music." Listen to this tropical-sounding, minor-key dance number—which veers even further from the standard thirty-two-bar structure than Arlen's "That Old Black Magic"—and you'll appreciate Richard Rodgers's remark that the popular composer who "has written the most enduring 'Jewish' music" is Porter, "an Episcopalian millionaire who was born on a farm in Peru, Indiana."

15.

"All of Me" (music, Gerald Marks; lyrics, Seymour Simons). Arrangement by George Siravo, November 7, 1946. Sinatra recorded this number many times, most notably on the *Swing Easy* album he did with Nelson Riddle's arrangements in 1953. That will remain the touchstone, but the Siravo version comes close, a sexy example of "kidding the lyrics." The singer's strut belies the words ("Your goodbye / left me with eyes that cry") and ends up sounding as belligerent as, say, "Why Should I Cry Over You?" Of numerous alternate takes, I like best the one that ends not with the Sinatra whistle but a mutter: "You better get it while you can, baby. I'm gettin' outta here."

16.

"My Romance" (Rodgers and Hart). April 25, 1947. Sinatra excelled at live duets during his radio years. He was up for a duet with anyone: opera singers (Lawrence Tibbett), actors (Van Johnson), the drummer Sy Oliver (who wrote "Yes, Indeed"), the Pied Pipers vocal group ("Somebody Loves Me"), and superb girl singers ranging from Eileen Barton ("Come Out, Wherever You Are") to Doris Day ("Let's Take an Old-Fashioned Walk"). Here he and Dinah Shore do justice to the lyric that states the rationale for popular music, namely that it can make fantastic dreams come true even when you're wide awake. How do you know it's a good duet? When the performers sound like they're genuinely having fun.

17.

"The Song Is You" (music, Jerome Kern; lyrics, Oscar Hammerstein II). October 26, 1947. Definitive version of a great standard.

18.

"Body and Soul" (music, Johnny Green; lyrics, Edward Heyman).* Recorded November 9, 1947, with Bobby Hackett on

---

*Though not credited, Howard Dietz, who collaborated with Arthur Schwartz on such songs as "That's Entertainment" and "I Guess I'll Have to Change My Plan," contributed to a lyric that can aptly be characterized as "noir."

trumpet. Music critic Gary Giddins calls this the best "straight" (i.e., non-jazz) rendition of a marvelous song whose release has been singled out—by jazz commentator Jamie Katz—as "the Golden Gate of musical bridges."

19.

"It All Depends on You" (Buddy DeSylva, Lew Brown, Ray Henderson). Recorded July 10, 1949, with Hugo Winterhalter's orchestra, and a fine sax solo from Wolfe Taninbaum. Sinatra does a little bebop scat following the bridge of this swing classic. Track five on *Swing and Dance with Frank Sinatra* is the best among many satisfactory takes. Compare with how Ruth Etting does this 1920s song—or how the greatly underrated Doris Day, playing Ruth Etting, does it on-screen in *Love Me or Leave Me*.

20.

"Bye Bye Baby" (music, Jule Styne; lyrics, Leo Robin). July 10, 1949. Swell brassy number from Jule Styne's *Gentlemen Prefer Blondes*. In the movie version, the song is a giant chorus number with solos by Jane Russell and Marilyn Monroe. Leo Robin's lyric cleverly transforms goodbye to its opposite through the agency of a pun: the song begins with the title phrase and ends with the lovers reunited: "I know that I'll be smiling / with my baby, by and by."

IT IS SEPTEMBER 9, 1945, a Sunday, and it's a wonderful day to be alive if you're Frank Sinatra on your way to a recording studio in Hollywood. You're still three months shy of your thirtieth birthday and you've done all the things that they write songs about. You've got the world on a string, and you've set it on fire. All's right with the world, too. One month ago the bombs fell on Hiroshima and Nagasaki, ending the war in the Pacific. The Japanese emperor said "the war situation has developed not necessarily to Japan's advantage." The invasion of Japan would not be necessary. And now peace was here, that elusive thing that you take for granted, like the air or the light of day, except when it is absent.

All the girls adore you. You're so skinny that comedians joke about it the way they'll someday joke about J-Lo's butt, though the best line in your defense will not be uttered until you begin your tempestuous affair with Ava Gardner, years from now. When director John Ford asks Ava to explain to a skeptic what she, the apotheosis of glamour, sees in "that hundred and twenty pound runt," Ava says, "He weighs a hundred and twenty, but a hundred and ten of those pounds are pure cock." But that is tomorrow's news. You will never have trouble getting the attention of the news media, from Walter Cronkite ("Mr. Believable") and *The New Yorker* to the tabloids of many cities around the globe. You will be the subject of biographies, hagiographies and hack jobs, documentaries and docudramas, gossip columns, FBI reports, conspiracy theories, high-toned essays of musical appreciation—the hero or villain of many *romans à clef* and of books in every genre, from *Why Sinatra Matters* to *Sinatraland* to *The Gospel According to Frank*. Someday a serious scholar will contend that "I'll Be Seeing You," one of your signature songs, was, in addition to being more popular in wartime than T. S. Eliot's *Four Quartets*, at least arguably a superior aesthetic experience.*

You have a great press agent (George Evans), a sympathetic record company executive (Manie Sacks), among other sharp advisers and persuasive advocates, and when you need a top-notch attorney, Mickey Rudin will walk into your life. You hire the best musicians. Arranger Axel Stordahl left the Dorsey band to join you when you went out on your own in 1942. Good choice. Words like "meteoric" or "irresistible" are standard adjectives for your rise. You will never again be the unknown kid you were once, never again enjoy the anonymity and privacy you could once take for granted. People surround you. You need police protection to get you through a worshipful crowd.

You wear those big floppy bow ties—Nancy's idea for concealing your prominent Adam's apple—and you had to laugh reading in the *New York Times* about the fashion trend you started, and how one male fashion editor growled that the reason for the growing demand for bow ties "wasn't Sinatra, you can be sure of that," it was just that men "got tired of wearing the same old ties."† Ha. You wanted to outdo Bing, and you're on your way.

You also want to take popular singing and make it an art,

---

*Paul Fussell, *Wartime* (New York: Oxford University Press, 1989), p. 253.
†"New Twists in Bow Ties," *New York Times*, August 19, 1945.

With lyricist Sammy Cahn, composer Jule Styne, and pianist Axel Stordahl.
Michael Ochs Archives / Getty Images

and this, too, you shall achieve: artistic greatness wedded to popular success. You know just how good you are, and you have balls. Before your first solo performance at the Paramount in New York City in 1943, you told Johnny and Ginny Mercer, "I'm going to sing Bing's ass off."

You have your own radio show. In 1945 alone you started with *Your Hit Parade*, then segued to *Max Factor Presents Frank Sinatra*, and now you're doing *Old Gold Presents Songs by Sinatra*. You know how hard it is to please Jerome Kern, and so it tickled you pink when he told you how much he liked your rendition of "Ol' Man River." "My idea with that song was to have a rabbity little fellow do it—somebody who made you believe he was tired of livin' and scared of dyin'. That's how you do it, Frankie."

Another thing: you have your own private songwriting team, Jule Styne for the music and Sammy Cahn for the words. Today you're going to record a number they wrote for the post-war effort: "Buy a Piece of the Peace." Back when you and Gene Kelly donned sailor suits for *Anchors Aweigh*, MGM said you could have anyone in Hollywood, even Kern, but you stood by the rookies. "If they're not there Monday, I won't be there Monday." You got your way. And a grin spread on your angular face. The *New York Times* reports that *Anchors Aweigh*—in which Kelly dances with a cartoon mouse and you sing "I Fall in Love Too Easily"—has been seen by 919,000 persons in its first eight weeks at the Capitol, a record, and is closing in on the ten-week mark set a year ago by *Since You Went Away*. They will be forever grateful, Cahn and Styne, writers of hit after hit for you, Frankie: "Saturday Night Is the Loneliest Night in the Week," "Come Out, Come Out, Wherever You Are," "Guess I'll Hang My Tears Out to Dry," "Five Minutes More," "Let

It Snow, Let It Snow, Let It Snow," "Time After Time." Their Oscar-winning "Three Coins in the Fountain" is still in the future. And even after Styne heads back to Broadway to compose the scores for *Gentlemen Prefer Blondes* and *Gypsy*, Sammy will stay in Hollywood and pair up with Jimmy Van Heusen—your old buddy, born Chester Babcock in Syracuse, who renamed himself after a shirt—and cahntinue (to use a favorite Sammy pun) to fashion not only your theme songs ("All the Way," "High Hopes," "Come Fly with Me," "Ring-a-Ding-Ding," "My Kind of Town") but the special parody lyrics you require to celebrate New Year's Eve, or Edward G. Robinson's birthday, or a presidential inauguration.

"I'll always write for Frank Sinatra whenever he asks me." Loyalty, thy name is Sammy Cahn.

26

SINATRA MADE NO apologies for his affiliation with night-club high rollers, tough guys, underworld bosses. But if you would know him by his associates, you must also consider his intimates: his wives and children, his glamorous lovers and playmates, costars and friends.

There was, of course, the Hollywood A-list, the Rat Pack, and some of the most beautiful women of the day. There were the strange political bedfellows of the Agnew years. There were the dedicated disc jockeys, the journalists and writers whose attitude toward Sinatra was diametrically opposite to those of the fault-finding Hearst columnists of the 1940s.

There was Hank Sincola, a Bronx street-fighting man, who (in Earl Wilson's words) "represented Frank fistically as well as fiscally." There were booze buddies like hard-drinking Jackie Gleason and Toots Shor of the famous midtown eatery. According to *Modern Drunkard* magazine, these two fast friends engaged in frequent drinking contests. When Jackie won, he ordered victory drinks for everybody. When Toots won, he left the passed-out body of Gleason on the floor as proof of his "Jewish drinking prowess." One time, Gleason, broke, borrowed a hundred bucks from Toots and blew it all on a limousine to take him and Sinatra to a nearby nightclub, where, impelled by what Poe had called "the imp of the perverse," he promptly borrowed another hundred and bribed the bandleader to play the same tune over and over while the audience looked bewildered and he guffawed.

In the same vein, there was Jilly Rizzo—companion, fellow prankster, bodyguard, and eventually the owner of Frank's favorite New York restaurant—and his second wife, Honey, whose azure hair got her the nickname "the blue Jew." A key scene in *The Manchurian Candidate* takes place at Jilly's. (Jilly's bartender, telling a story, says, "Why don't you go and take yourself a cab and go up to Central Park and go jump in the lake?" and the character played by Laurence Harvey, who has been hypnotically conditioned to obey commands, proceeds to do just that.) Johnny Carson was a Jilly's habitué. When Sinatra made an entrance, everything stopped. One night Johnny and Ed McMahon were sitting at the piano bar when in walked Sinatra. "Everyone just watched in reverence as His Holiness walked past the bar," McMahon recalled. "No one would dare speak to him unless he spoke first. No one wanted to be turned into salt. And then, throughout the restaurant the voice of Johnny Carson was heard: 'Dammit, Frank,' he said, 'I told you ten-thirty!' "

Sinatra admired professionalism and expertise in any area; among his friends was the certified bookworm Bennett Cerf, head of Random House, whom he fondly dubbed "the Bookmaker." Another friend was America's most celebrated cardiovascular surgeon, the pioneering Dr. Michael DeBakey. Above all there was the fellowship of musicians he admired— and the veneration of musicians who admired him, beginning with the category of "vocalists, popular," extending to jazz and swing and Brazilian *bossa nova* (Antonio Carlos Jobim), branching out to Bob Dylan, Paul McCartney, David Bowie, and even the Sex Pistols, who covered "My Way" in their way. And let us not leave out the longtime manager of the Los Angeles Dodgers, Tom Lasorda, who liked nothing better than to have Sinatra in the clubhouse with a big bowl of pasta before a game. Sinatra shared exclusive box seats at Dodger Stadium with Cary Grant and Gregory Peck.

SINATRA HAD A right to feel pretty damn good as he prepared for his gig with the *Treasury Department Music for Millions Show* on September 9, 1945. He had offered his services without compensation. Sammy and Jule had written a new song, and there would be a full orchestra and a lot of brass supporting Frank, who always loved singing with a big band behind him. "Buy a Piece of the Peace" was a plea to the public to buy a new issue of war bonds. Today a commercial for bonds might stress their yield or their safety. But "Buy a Piece of the Peace" made its appeal on patriotic and pacific grounds. Dig deep down, do your part, please don't cease. After all, there are war-torn lands "we must police." Sinatra makes it sound like he wants just five minutes more in your arms, and I swear if you heard that song today, with its big brassy bridge, you would recognize it for what it is: brilliant songwriting, completely of a piece with the other great Styne-and-Cahn creations of that era, like "I've Heard That Song Before," and maybe you'd smile at the thought that the Treasury Department was relying for its revenue on the work of a couple of Jewish songwriters and an Italian-American kid from Hoboken.

UNLIKE CLARK GABLE, who flew bombing missions, or bandleader Glenn Miller, who lost his life on a trip to entertain the troops in Europe, Sinatra stayed out of uniform; he went abroad for his first USO tour only after Germany had surrendered. To irate right-wing columnists Westbrook Pegler and Lee Mortimer, Sinatra's 4-F status (on the grounds of a punctured eardrum, possibly a consequence of a boyhood fight) was just one in a series of reasons for righteous resentment. Here was this skinny, arrogant non-soldier making the lonely girls swoon while the real heroes were risking their lives battling formidable foes in Europe, North Africa, and the Pacific. A young man at a Sinatra concert had thrown eggs at the singer, several of which hit their target in the face. (Tabloid headline: "Hen Fruit Hits Heartthrob.") The historian William Manchester famously speculated that "Sinatra was the most hated man of World War II, much more than Hitler," and Frank anticipated a cool reception from the GIs in Italy. Luckily Frank counted the comedian Phil Silvers among his friends, and when they did their act, Silvers turned his jokes about the singer's weight ("I know there's a food shortage, but this is ridiculous") to the singer's advantage. The strategy worked. "He had those boys in the palm of his skinny hand."

On the same trip Sinatra got to meet Pope Pius XII in the Vatican. Incensed about Father Coughlin's anti-Semitic radio rants, broadcast nationally out of Detroit, Sinatra was determined to confront the pontiff on the matter. "Wait till I tell off that Pope," Sinatra told Silvers. When he entered the papal presence he thought better of it, however, and when the pope asked him what he sang he replied earnestly with a list of song titles starting with "Ol' Man River." Pope Pius looked puzzled; he had merely been wondering whether Frank was a tenor, a baritone, or a bass.*

Back in the States, Frank came out strongly in favor of religious and racial tolerance. You can't fake the sincerity in his voice when he sang about what America meant to him. *The House I Live In* includes grocers and butchers, "the worker by my side" of whatever race, religion, or national origin. It's like a thirty-two-bar version of Whitman's vision of America in "Song of Myself." In the movie, a short, for which he would win an honorary Oscar in 1946, Frank stops a gang of urban youngsters from beating up a Jewish boy. How does he do it? By saying that bigotry makes sense only to "a Nazi or somebody as stupid"—and by singing the title song, an ode to American democracy written by a couple of leftist visionaries, Earl Robinson (music) and Lewis Allan (lyrics): "The 'howdy' and the handshake, the air of feeling free / And the right to speak my mind out, that's America to me."†

---

*There are other versions of this anecdote, but central to all that I have encountered is a misunderstanding of this sort between pontiff and popular singer.

†Earl Robinson was blacklisted in 1945. Lewis Allan was the pen name of Abel Meeropol, who, with his wife, adopted the Rosenberg children after their parents were executed. The song seems unimpeachably patriotic—Sinatra sang it at Reagan's second inaugural, in 1985—yet in the 1940s was considered by conservative columnists to be unmistakably pinko, possibly because of the favorable reference to "the worker by my side" and the inclusion of "all races and religions."

Sinatra tried doing the same thing real time in autumn 1945 when the white students of Froebel High School in Gary, Indiana, went on strike to protest their principal's "pro-Negro" policies. The new principal had declared that the school's 270 black kids were entitled to participate in student government and could use the school's swimming pool one day a week. Frank went out to Gary to give the assembled high school kids a lesson in tolerance. Reporting on the event, *Life* magazine deplored the "childish grievances" of the white protesters and implicated their parents, "who feared competition for their steel-mill jobs from Gary's increasing Negro population." But the magazine could hardly restrain its glee at the outcome. "When it was all over, Frankie had failed. The strike was still on." Well, fuck you, scumbag. I don't see what *you're* doing to improve the relations of white and black, Jew and gentile. Goddamn press always did get under his skin.

29

HEARST COLUMNIST LEE Mortimer never tired of disparaging Sinatra and his fans. The singer was a shirker and a "left-winger." According to Mortimer, Sinatra managed the difficult feat of being both a Commie and a hood: "The Communists and the gangsters both have the same motive, acquiring respectability by association with prestige names." (On the ideological incompatibility of the groups in question, consider the joke that the mobster Barzini makes to appreciative laughter when the heads of the crime families meet at Don Corleone's behest in *The Godfather*: "Certainly, he can present a bill for [his] services. After all, we are not Communists.") To Mortimer, the screaming girls were "squealing, shouting neurotic extremists." Sinatra didn't entertain the troops until after hostilities had ceased. *The House I Live In* was merely propaganda for "class struggle or foreign isms posing as entertainment." And furthermore, he got where he did because of Willie Moretti in New Jersey and the Fischetti brothers, who got him off the hook with Dorsey, and didn't he deliver a couple of million bucks to Lucky Luciano in Havana? When Sinatra punched out Mortimer at Ciro's on April 8, 1947—allegedly because "he called me a dirty dago son of a bitch, and I wouldn't take that from anyone"—he was striking a blow for artists everywhere who are misunderstood by malignant critics. Unfortunately for him, it was a nail in the coffin of his image as the shy fellow and good family man with the wife from the old neighborhood. The second and third nails were provided by (*a*) the circulation of a photo of Sinatra, allegedly a bag man for Lucky Luciano, arriving in Havana, and (*b*) his affair with Ava Gardner. (And what an affair it was.)

But the Lee Mortimer episode is a fascinating, even horrifying, footnote, if only for something that happened years later. When he heard that Mortimer was dead, Sinatra found out where the columnist was buried. Then, after a few drinks, he got Brad Dexter and some other buddies to accompany him to the cemetery, where they could witness him pissing on the late cocksucker's grave.

30

IN THE HOLLYWOOD version of *Guys and Dolls* (1955), Marlon Brando plays Sky Masterson and Sinatra plays Nathan Detroit. Conventional wisdom has it that both men are miscast, because Masterson has to do more singing and Brando does not have the better singing voice. I happen to like Sinatra's performance as Nathan Detroit, who runs "the oldest established permanent floating crap game in New York." It's a persona he would relish (and reanimate) in the first of the Rat Pack movies, *Ocean's Eleven* (1960), a comic caper in which Sinatra and company (Dean Martin, Sammy Davis, Jr., Peter Lawford, Joey Bishop, Richard Conte, et al.) conspire to rob five Las Vegas casinos simultaneously at midnight on New Years' Eve. In *Ocean's Eleven*, Angie Dickinson, playing Sinatra's estranged wife, tells him that he "could never love a woman the way you love danger." What he leads is "not a life, it's a floating crap game."

The role of Danny Ocean was the third Danny he played in his film career. Each of the roles corresponds to an aspect of the actor's life.

In *It Happened in Brooklyn* (1947), he plays Danny Miller, a homesick World War II veteran who carries in his wallet a picture not of a girlfriend or screen siren but of the Brooklyn Bridge. He also sings "The Brooklyn Bridge" and five other vintage Jule Styne and Sammy Cahn songs, including "Time After Time," "I Believe," and "It's the Same Old Dream." Danny Miller is a working-class guy—sensitive, innocent, and

Wary rivals: with Brando in *Guys and Dolls*.
Ullstein Bild / Getty Images

shy, in line with Sinatra's 1940s persona. He's back in his beloved Brooklyn, but it's rougher than he expected it to be. He's
a shipping clerk who wants to be a singer, and you can bet he
will get the music scholarship he covets, because he has learned
from Jimmy Durante that "The Song's Gotta Come from the
Heart." In their duet, Sinatra does an imitation of Durante that
Variety said was "sockeroo." Frankie was still golden.

As Danny Wilson in *Meet Danny Wilson* (1951), however,
Sinatra is a club singer who loses his girlfriend (Shelley Win-
ters) to his best friend (Alex Nicol) and loses his best friend to
a bullet fired by mobster Nick Driscoll (Raymond Burr), who
owns the club where Danny sings and is more of an extortion-
ist than an employer. (Recalling to mind a certain trombone-
playing bandleader from Sinatra's own past, Nick has a contract
with Danny that entitles him to fifty percent of the vocalist's
earnings, past and present.) Only the last-minute arrival of
the police saves Danny from himself, for in a fit of a rage and
revenge, the two-time loser has set out to avenge his friend's
murder. Released when Sinatra was on the skids—when he
lacked a recording studio, a movie contract, a faithful wife, a
worshipful audience, and a press that was not overtly hostile—
the movie is almost an allegory of Sinatra's career arc at that
particular moment. In one scene, Danny Wilson, who once
sang to the happy shrieks of adolescent girls, is drunk, his head
down on the bar, when a girl puts a nickel into the machine and
out comes Danny's own rendition of "When You're Smiling."
If Sinatra's career had come to an unhappy ending, this is where
you'd find him. Though he sings "That Old Black Magic,"
"She's Funny That Way," "All of Me," and a couple of other
standards, the film flopped.

But that was long ago, and here Danny Ocean stands, a man

among the heroic men of the 82nd Airborne Division: a band of brothers proud of their derring-do in World War II. As Karen McNally puts it in her study of Sinatra's movies, *When Frankie Went to Hollywood: Frank Sinatra and American Male Identity* (2008), in *Ocean's Eleven*, "Sinatra's virile excess is no longer tempered . . . by expressions of emotional vulnerability." As in *It Happened in Brooklyn*, Sinatra plays a veteran in *Ocean's Eleven*. (For a man who did not serve in the military, Frank is often in uniform—in a sailor suit with Gene Kelly in the 1940s, in an army uniform in *From Here to Eternity*, *The Manchurian Candidate*, and *Von Ryan's Express*—or is identified as a veteran, as in *Some Came Running*.) In *Ocean's Eleven* he portrays a successful playboy, gambler, and man-about-town. Still, some familiar crises lurk beneath the surface. Danny Ocean's marriage is falling apart, and what motivates him and company to rob the casinos of Las Vegas is not avarice so much as the lure of the great dare: the desire to recapture what cannot be recaptured—the adventure, the romance, the virility of youth.

UNTIL HE WAS thirty-four years old and adversity gave him a taste of its medicine, Sinatra was a boy, by which I mean he was not just a big band boy singer, like Bob Eberly or Dick Haymes, but a boy in a man's world, a golden boy to be sure, and one who was cruising for a comeuppance. The difference was Ava Gardner. Their love affair taught him how to sing a torch song and mean every word of it, to sing it with full belief and total credibility. "That's how he learned," Nelson Riddle told Kitty Kelley. "She was the greatest love of his life, and he lost her."

"Hurricane Ava"—as gossip queen Louella Parsons put it—was the glorious femme fatale in the melodrama of Frank Sinatra's life. "When Frank met Ava, it was like atomic fusion. There was a terrific explosion, tremendous damage and long-lasting fallout."

Who was this magnificent creature who was capable of putting an end to the enduring partnership of a forgiving wife and a cheating husband? She was a sharecropper's daughter from North Carolina whose dark beauty landed her a fifty-dollar-a-week contract with MGM in 1941 when she was eighteen. She went from rags to superstardom and was a tigress on and off the screen. When she played a dancer in *The Barefoot Contessa* (1954), MGM promoted her as "the world's most beautiful animal."

Courtship: one night in Palm Springs Frank and Ava got drunk and went on a rampage in his car, shooting out the streetlights in town and a bunch of shop windows with the two .38s he kept in his glove compartment.

Ava was reaching the height of her fame at the same time as Frank was losing his footing. Louella Parsons, whom Gore Vidal called "the Saint-Simon of San Simeon," observes that "Frank wasn't philandering now; he was deadly serious. A woman can . . . handle a dozen rivals, but I never knew a woman who could handle just one." Nancy Barbato Sinatra threw in the towel and got her divorce on October 30, 1951. Then lady luck followed Nancy out the door. Sinatra was having voice problems. He faced an unsympathetic boss at Columbia Records. Worst of all, as Louella Parsons wrote, "he wasn't Frank Sinatra anymore; he was Ava Gardner's husband."

"Frank was flat broke when we tied the knot," Ava told author Peter Evans, approaching him to ghost her memoir even though she and Frank had vowed never to write their autobiographies. "I don't know where those stories came from that the Mafia was taking care of him. They should have been. But the fucking so-called Family was nowhere to be seen when he needed them. It really ticks me when I read how generous the Mob was when he was on the skids. But I was the one paying the rent when he couldn't get arrested. I was the one making the pot boil, baby. It was *me*!"*

Ava once threw a glass of champagne at a cameraman, and even he thought she was "so bloody gorgeous" as the glass and its contents were flying at him. That was the effect Ava Gardner had. Like a hurricane, but beautiful, glamorous yet earthy, she could swear like a sailor; had a terrible temper; gravitated

*Peter Evans, *Ava Gardner: The Secret Conversations*. New York: Simon & Schuster, 2013. The conversations were held in 1988.

naturally to macho men, matadors, crooners, big band leaders, big-game-hunting American writers on safari. She was five foot six, a stunning brunette with a pleasing voice. In the movie *Show Boat* (1951) they dubbed in a professional singer to cover her musical numbers (a bad move; it sounds phony), but on the soundtrack album it's all Ava. Her voice full of tequila cocktails was just right for Julie's showstopper "Bill." She posed for Man Ray, who found her "absolutely ravishing." During the filming of *The Barefoot Contessa* in Rome, a sculptor got her to step out of her little two-piece, one piece at a time. He did inspired work. Though the posing and the sculpture were part of the plot, they used a statue in which the model is dressed, not the life-size nude, in the movie. (*Damn it, it has tits*, an executive roared.) Sinatra bought it, brought it to California, and eventually planted the statue in the garden of his house in Coldwater Canyon.

Ava commanded an unusual loyalty. Among her ex-husbands, Sinatra had hot nuts for her as for no other. The naked statue stood supreme until Frank's fourth wife, Barbara Marx, made him take it down. When Ava fell ill in 1989, Frank paid all the bills. He called her "Angel." But he didn't attend the funeral when she died in January 1990. Neither did her two other ex-husbands, Mickey Rooney (a mistake when she was nineteen and breaking into the business) and clarinetist heartthrob Artie Shaw (who ruined her self-esteem by reminding her how uneducated she was). Mickey Rooney remembered that sex with her had been great. "Not for me," she demurred. She was the same height as Catherine Deneuve (5 foot 6 inches); her eyebrows and mouth rivaled Vivien Leigh's; her eyes gave Elizabeth Taylor's a run for the money. (Liz Taylor is "not beautiful—she is pretty," Ava told an influential publisher. "*I* was beautiful.") On the sexuality scale, Ava ranked right up there with Marilyn Monroe, Rita Hayworth, and Kim Novak. She was a Capricorn with Cancer rising, her moon and Mars in Pisces, Venus in Scorpio, and Mercury in Capricorn. In Chinese astrology, she was a water dog. She taught Frank heartbreak and the dark side of passion. Sinatra put all the misery of his relationship with Ava into "I'm a Fool to Want You" (which he recorded first with the Ray Charles Singers on March 27, 1951), a lonely masterpiece that came out of the nadir of his career. When, on later albums, he sings "I Get Along Without You Very Well" or "Angel Eyes" or "Blues in the Night," you know he's thinking of Ava.

As for Ava's point of view, two songs state it directly. "Between the Devil and the Deep Blue Sea" (music, Harold Arlen; lyrics, Ted Koehler) presents the basic antithesis: "I don't want you, / but I hate to lose you." And these lines from "You Took Advantage of Me" (Rodgers and Hart) sum up precisely how she felt about her third husband: "I suffer something awful each time you go, / and much worse when you're near."

32

AVA AND FRANK became an item in 1949, the year that *On the Town* was filmed with Sinatra, Gene Kelly, and Jules Munshin as the three navy sailors on twenty-four-hour shore leave in New York City. In the time-honored tradition of the Hollywood in-joke—as when Cary Grant refers to "Archie Leach," or Tom Ewell is accused of harboring Marilyn Monroe behind a closed door—Ava is name-checked in the film: when a pretty girl floats by the three sailors like a melody and Kelly looks unimpressed, Munshin says, "Who you got waiting for you in New York, Ava Gardner?"

Ava and Frank tied the knot eight days after Nancy got her decree of divorce in 1951, but it was no honeymoon. The couple's bitter quarrels added to the sexual intensity of the relationship. The pattern repeated itself with variations: he would pursue her, woo her; they would reconcile and have the world's greatest makeup sex; and as soon as the postcoital cigarettes were stubbed out, the bickering would begin anew.

"We would be sitting in the living room and hear them upstairs in the bedroom quarreling and arguing. Ava would scream at Frank and he would slam the door and storm downstairs. Minutes later we'd smell a very sweet fragrance coming from the stairs. Ava had decided she wasn't mad anymore, and so she sprayed the stairwell with her perfume. Frank would smell it and race back up to the bedroom. Then it would be hours before he'd come back down."*

A Sinatra exit line during one of his fights with Ava: "Swell. You just go off with your sister, and I'll be in Palm Springs fucking Lana Turner."

From the start, people had warned Ava about Frank. Why didn't she listen? "He was good in the feathers. You don't pay much attention to what other people tell you when a guy's good in the feathers," she said. And, in the same vein, "We were always great in bed. The trouble usually started on the way to the bidet."

*Betty Burns, wife of Sinatra's manager at the time, quoted by Kitty Kelley, *His Way*, p. 141.

33

BOTH FRANK AND Bing were influenced greatly by jazz. Both partnered off with a dancer (Crosby with Fred Astaire, Sinatra with Gene Kelly). They were rivals in the way DiMaggio and Ted Williams were rivals. But they liked each other and harmonized wonderfully. Crosby sang the low notes, Sinatra the high, making them ideal partners. I particularly recommend the medley of three songs they performed with John Scott Trotter's orchestra on a Crosby television show in the 1950s: "Among My Souvenirs," "September Song," and "As Time Goes By."

Crosby always sounded reassuring, even when singing the ballad of the Depression years, "Brother, Can You Spare a Dime?" and all the more so when courting the girls in a song like "Did You Ever See a Dream Walking?" Crosby was tuneful, pleasant, polite. Not Sinatra: there was always danger there. Something erotic, something scary. Passion, longing, desire that could turn into murderous anger or suicidal anguish.

The young Sinatra sang with ease, though never quite as effortlessly as Crosby. He could soften his voice miraculously and scoop up a low note with verve—like the last note in the phrase "you can be better than you are" from "Swinging on a Star," a Crosby hit, which won the Academy Award and which sounds a little like a Boy Scout song when Bing sang it with the kids, but cool when Sinatra sang it on a stage in 1946.

Crosby kept a distance between himself and his material. He sang with marvelous insouciance, and when the melodic line dipped into a low valley, as it does on "Mountain Greenery" and "Jeepers Creepers," no one is smoother than Bing (though Dick Haymes comes close). Sinatra can do insouciance on his up-tempo songs, or on family-friendly fare like "Love and Marriage" and "High Hopes," but when the element of drama is present, Sinatra sings from the heart, gets involved in the lyrics, projects the illusion of sincerity, intimacy.

Nothing could more dramatically convey the difference between the singers than their treatment of "Ol' Man River." In 1928, a year after the song was introduced in *Show Boat*, Crosby recorded it with the Paul Whiteman Orchestra—Bix Beiderbecke and Jimmy Dorsey among the instrumentalists—with a Dixieland flavor. Crosby sang it fast. In 1943, Sinatra sang it at the Hollywood Bowl, giving it the full dramatic treatment. There is a miraculous moment at the end of the bridge, a moment when most singers pause for breath before launching into the final stanza, which climbs an octave and a half from start to finish. Not Sinatra. He sustains the last note of the bridge—on the word "jail," which is where you land when you get drunk on Saturday night—across two bars so that it melts into the first word of the final stanza: "I get weary . . ." He also sustains the first syllable of "along," the last word in the song, seemingly beyond human endurance. It is an amazing vocal feat, but what is most noteworthy about it is the level of dramatic intensity. It made Louis B. Mayer cry, and on the strength of that performance, Mayer signed the lad to a five-year contract with MGM.

In the movie tribute to Jerome Kern, *Till the Clouds Roll By*, in which Robert Walker is Kern and Van Heflin plays his fictional friend and mentor, the composer's songs are rendered by various MGM stars. The last is Sinatra, in a white tuxedo, as if on the top of a wedding cake, rising to vocal heights when, surrounded by musicians, he sings "Ol' Man River." Conventional wisdom has it that the scene is a mistake, sartorially and otherwise. I say: Just listen.

IN A 2003 piece in London's *Times Literary Supplement*, critic Clive James riffed on the differences between Crosby and Sinatra as extrapolated from their roles in *High Society* (1956), the Cole Porter movie musical based on *The Philadelphia Story*, with Crosby, Grace Kelly, and Sinatra in the roles originally played by Cary Grant, Katharine Hepburn, and Jimmy Stewart, respectively. "Sinatra had been doing his best for years to divert the traditional repertoire in the direction of actual sexual passion, rather than well-behaved self-control. Bing stood for adulthood, with all its renunciations. Sinatra stood for adultery." It did not escape James's attention that a big Sinatra hit was "Love and Marriage," which he sang in a made-for-television production of Thornton Wilder's *Our Town*. James writes, "When, in 'Love and Marriage,' he sang that they went together like a horse and carriage, you could tell he thought that the sentiment was a natural product of the horse." Bing, come to think of it, "would probably have agreed with Sinatra on the subject but would never have let himself be caught uttering a non-conformist nuance. Sinatra's problem was that nuances were as far as he could go. In the world of the well-made song, illicit love, no matter how delicious, was a crime, and the compulsion to sing about it was the punishment."

Pete Hamill puts the same thought more pungently in *Why Sinatra Matters*: as singers, Sinatra was "almost always the lover," while Crosby was "the reigning husband."

NOT THE BOY singer's virtuosity but the mature baritone of Sinatra in the 1950s and sixties, roughened with bourbon and sleepless nights, the cost of high living and heartbreak—this is our public voice, the surrogate voice of the man in the street, the fan. It is the voice of cities and heroes but also that of the average Joe, the mutt, the drunk in the saloon.

During the Capitol years (1953–61), and the Reprise years that followed, Sinatra's voice is no longer quite as impressive or as naturally pleasing as when he performed at the Paramount and recorded for the Columbia label. It has lost range, ease, precision; he now has to work for his high notes. The voice that sounded pretty has "been through the mill of love," to borrow Cole Porter's phrase. It has grown deeper and fuller with experience—experience as processed with the aid of whiskey and a ritual cigarette. "The cigarettes you light, one after another, / Won't help you forget her, or the way that you love her" ("Learnin' the Blues"). "So drink up, all you people" ("Angel Eyes"). "I hope you didn't mind my bending your ear" ("One for My Baby"). All the boyishness that showed in the songs he recorded with the Harry James and Tommy Dorsey bands is gone. The paradox is that Sinatra in the 1950s hasn't as great a voice, and yet is a greater singer. He sounds unconstrained, free, less sweet, more real. This is evident in his assured mastery of fast tempos in such Nelson Riddle–arranged masterpieces as *Songs for Swingin' Lovers!*

(1956) and *A Swingin' Affair* (1957). Has anyone ever sounded as authentically joyous as Sinatra in "I've Got the World on a String"? The inventor of his own casual, finger-snapping style, he seems now also uncannily gifted at turning a song into ersatz autobiography, as when he tries to fool himself that he "get[s] along without you very well," or confides that he is "irresponsible," reflects that love, like youth, may be wasted on the young, reminisces about riding in the limousines of rich women when he was thirty-five, hangs his tears out to dry because he saw "her" on the street and she passed him right by, or confesses that he still feels "lucky to be loving you."

Sinatra has, you might say, a talent for narrative. He turns a thirty-two-bar song into a short story, usually a love story, told from the heights of romantic excitement ("I've Got the World on a String"), the depths of romantic despair ("I'm a Fool to Want You"), with buoyancy ("You Make Me Feel So Young"), or defiance ("That's Life"), or melancholy ("Last Night When We Were Young"), or the promise of an amorous adventure ("Let's Fall in Love"). Each song feels like a chapter—or sometimes just a brief episode—in the life.

A few years ago, I had lunch with Julius La Rosa, the talented boy singer on Arthur Godfrey's radio and TV shows in the early 1950s until the host unforgivably fired the singer on the air. Julius chose Sinatra's version of "I Get a Kick Out of You" to illustrate the singer's narrative approach. "He sang the song not as it is written, not as a band (or dance) song, but as a song with a story to tell," La Rosa said. "He put a comma here, a period there." La Rosa also told me that in his estimation Sinatra was number one, and that the next-best singer "was number thirty-seven."

Quite a few songs—starting with "My Way" and "New

York, New York"—are identified with Sinatra rather than with the song's writers. Thus we have records like Bob Dylan's *Shadows of the Night* (2015), featuring such perennials as "Why Try to Change Me Now?" and the little-known gem "Stay with Me"; or Tony Bennett's *Perfectly Frank* (1992), which includes an unusual up-tempo cover of "One for My Baby." A favorite CD of mine, *Blue Note Plays Sinatra* (1995), consists of jazz treatments of Sinatra songs. There's Freddie Hubbard with "All or Nothing at All," Dexter Gordon with "Guess I'll Hang My Tears Out to Dry," Sonny Rollins with "I've Got You under My Skin," the Three Sounds with "Witchcraft" and "It Was a Very Good Year," Jacky Terrasson with "I Love Paris," Miles Davis with "It Never Entered My Mind," Ike Quebec with "Nancy (with the Laughing Face)," Bennie Green with "This Love of Mine," and Joe Lovano with "Angel Eyes."* In what sense are these Sinatra songs? Except for "This Love of Mine," for which he wrote lyrics, Sinatra wrote none of them; but he sang them so well that the majority of titles in this paragraph are forever associated with him. And the list is far from complete.

You can say that Sinatra, in this very specific sense, owns "The Song Is You" and "Come Fly with Me," "The Best Is Yet to Come" and "Summer Wind."† Some of these songs were

---

*Also on the disc are Art Blakey and the Jazz Messengers with "Come Rain or Come Shine" and Cannonball Adderley with "Dancing in the Dark." Although Sinatra does them well, these songs do not belong to him in the same sense as, for example, "Witchcraft" (music by Cy Coleman, lyrics by Carolyn Leigh), which, with a Nelson Riddle arrangement, Sinatra released as a single in 1957. It got a lot of air time, climbed up the charts and stayed there, and was nominated for Grammy Awards in several categories in May 1959, the first year that Grammys were given.

†That doesn't prevent others from singing them, of course. (The contrary is the case.) It just means that Sinatra got there first or made a big hit of it. The

written specifically for Sinatra to sing. But Cole Porter wrote "I've Got You under My Skin," the Gershwins wrote "A Foggy Day" and "They Can't Take That Away from Me," Rodgers and Hart wrote "The Lady Is a Tramp," Harold Arlen and Ted Koehler wrote "I've Got the World on a String," Arlen and Yip Harburg wrote "Last Night When We Were Young," and Buddy DeSylva and his partners wrote "It All Depends on You" before they had ever heard of Frank—and yet these are undeniably Sinatra songs through and through. Seldom can a performing (or interpretive) artist lay claim to such an almost authorial relationship to material someone else has composed. And yet, let it be noted, Sinatra made it a practice to acknowledge the songwriters, and often the arrangers, of each song he sang in live performance.

---

number on the Sinatra list is staggering. Think of such outstanding talents as Vic Damone, Jack Jones, Bobby Darin, Dean Martin, and Tony Bennett and the number of songs each of them can be said to "own." The truth is, Sinatra never had any real competition after Crosby. And time, which has made Crosby sound dated, has had no such effect on Sinatra.

36

"I DISCOVERED VERY early that my instrument wasn't my voice," Sinatra said. "It was the microphone." It was the microphone that put paid to Al Jolson's preeminence. It was the microphone that allowed you to lower your voice to a whisper. When you don't have to belt a song, when your unassisted voice doesn't have to reach the last rows of the theater, you can enunciate more clearly and you have greater vocal control. Pete Hamill says that Sinatra thought of himself "as a musician whose instrument was the microphone."

Jonathan Schwartz opines that "Bing Crosby's greatest piece of luck" was "that he came of age with the microphone," while Sinatra's luck lay in "the advent of the long-playing album, a format that would allow him to string together miniature works to create a specific mood on a broader canvas. It was now possible to include sixteen songs on a phonograph record, with a novelist's scope and vision."

For many listeners, *In the Wee Small Hours* is not only the first but the greatest of his concept albums. The jacket depicts the singer's persona: he stands with tie loosened, a lighted cigarette in his right hand, his fedora pushed back on his head, his thin face with the prominent curved eyebrows. The mood is pensive, melancholic. It's nighttime. The city street is empty except for the singer, and would be dark except for the illumination of streetlamps. He stands beneath one, as if it were a friend. There are three Rodgers and Hart songs on the album:

"It Never Entered My Mind," "Dancing on the Ceiling," and "Glad to Be Unhappy." The first of these may be the best thing on the record, unless that distinction goes to Harold Arlen's "Last Night When We Were Young" (with lyrics by Yip Harburg), or Hoagy Carmichael's "I Get Along Without You Very Well," or possibly Cole Porter's "What Is This Thing Called Love?" or Duke Ellington's "Mood Indigo." I think you get the point.

Sinatra has concept albums devoted to moonlight, travel, dancing, swing music, "swing" as a style of living, Tommy Dorsey, Antonio Carlos Jobim, and the dark despair that only the lonely know.

37

BOSOM BUDDIES. DEAN would call Frank "Pally" or "Dago"—as in "Dago, it's time for bed," because Martin wanted to sleep and get up early to play golf, while Sinatra was still shaking down the stars at three in the morning.

Sinatra wasn't all that taken with Martin when he caught the Martin and Lewis nightclub act in June 1948: "The dago's lousy, but the little Jew is great." That view changed when both Frank and Dean were under contract to Capitol in the 1950s. The friendship grew to the point where Hollywood photographer Sid Avery said: "They'd have killed for each other. I'm not altogether sure they didn't."

The parallels in the careers of Sinatra and Dean Martin are not often discussed, though their friendship and professional collaborations are toasted and talked about.

Like Sinatra, Martin had to make a dramatic comeback. After the breakup of Martin and Lewis, the most successful comic act in America, Dino was in a funk. His life of lucrative moviemaking contracts and nightclub engagements had come to an abrupt end. No one thought he had a chance to make it as a singer, an actor, or as the host of one of the most popular TV shows of the 1960s and early seventies. That lay in the future. For the moment, Dean was up to his ears in debt, and his prospects were slim to none.

Like Sinatra in *From Here to Eternity*, Martin puts on a uniform in his comeback film, *The Young Lions*, where the

Frank's friendship with Dean Martin ran longer
than any of his marriages.

Allan Grant / Getty Images

headliners are Marlon Brando and Montgomery Clift but where Dino gives an altogether convincing performance as a vain entertainer who wants to dodge the draft and ends up a military hero at the Bulge alongside Clift, the same tormented Monty who acted alongside Frank in *Eternity*.

A short time later, Martin read that Frank was looking for a guy to play a blackjack dealer in his next film. Dean thought, *Hell, I smoke, drink, and play cards. I wouldn't even have to act.* "Frank laughed and said, 'What do you know? You're right.' He hired me on the spot" for *Some Came Running*, another important moment in the resurrection of Dean Martin's career.

By 1967 Dean had it made in the shade: he was making Matt Helm movies, comedies, and westerns, cutting records, cutting up on TV, making a lot of dough. *Newsweek* punned that he was "King Leer." And he and Frank were best friends forever.

That said, let's ponder the differences between the two.

Begin with the fact that Dean, aloof, liked being left alone, whereas Frank liked having a gang of guys around him. Frank blurred the line between art and life; Dean kept them in separate compartments. The drunk act, for example: Dean drank Martinelli's apple juice, the color of scotch, on stage. (Said Frank, "I spill more than Dean drinks.") Where Sinatra was ever restless and allergic to being alone, Dean Martin wanted to get a good night's sleep. He threw a joint party for his daughter Deana (who was turning eighteen) and for the actress Jill St. John. The pop group Buffalo Springfield (lead singer Stephen Stills) was hired to perform. The party, Deana writes, was "fantastic" until the police came to break it up because neighbors complained about the noise. It wasn't a neighbor who called. It was Dean.

Both Sinatra and Martin were great entertainers, talented actors. But one is really a singer at heart, the other a comic genius.

The reason Sinatra is a superior singer is the same reason that he is not as talented a comedian as his best buddy. One night at the Sands they decided to flip roles. Sinatra got all of Dean's cracks, and Dean got the straight-man lines. And still Dean got more laughs. Frank: "How come no one's laughing at me?" Dean: "Because you're just not funny." Deana Martin diplomatically says that Uncle Frank was "very funny," but that her father was "a natural." She's right about her dad, but Dean was right about Frank: he was too serious, too intense, too dramatic, *too much* to be funny. If he got drunk enough he would do his Jimmy Cagney imitation ("You dirty rat"), which was even less funny than Jimmy Stewart imitating Cagney and sounding like Jimmy Stewart.

Sometimes Dean sacrificed music to theater, song to jest. He would begin a song: "You Made Me Love You." And then, just when we're expecting "you didn't have to do it," he would sing "you woke me up to do it." Or he would take the Rodgers & Hart classic that goes "You are too beautiful for one man alone," and continue, in the proper meter, with: "so I brought along my brother."

The wit came naturally to Dean, who couldn't take himself, or the entertainment racket, with high seriousness. Gifted with a baritone that was a bridge between the manner of Bing and that of Elvis, Dean could sing love songs beautifully. "Everybody Loves Somebody" displaced the Beatles at the top of the charts in 1964. He may have the best recording out there of "Just in Time." And I have a great weakness for the songs he did with real or faux Italian: "That's Amore," "Volare," "On an Evening in Roma." But Dean could never do the "Soliloquy" from *Carousel*, or "Ol' Man River" from *Show Boat*, or "Where's My Bess?" from *Porgy and Bess*, or even "That's Life," and certainly not the song that begins "What is America to me?" All of these Frank sang for full dramatic effect. And it is not a question entirely of vocal range or power. Depending on your point of view, Dean lacked either the grandiloquence or the gravitas, or maybe he was just unwilling to suspend his sense of irony.

Sinatra—who couldn't tell a joke to save his life, although the audience loved him and therefore laughed when he tried, just as they generously supplied the words to "The Second Time Around" when in a late concert he went up on the lines— had a self-conception that allowed him to sing songs of utmost seriousness, songs that brought a hush to the audience. He believed every word of "The House I Live In," which he sang at the White House for Kennedy, Nixon, and Reagan. No reflexive irony stood in the way.

In 1953, Sinatra made what one of his biographers called four "suicide gestures." One night, for example, Ava Gardner heard a gunshot and raced into Frank's room. His body was lying across the bed, but he was all right; he had fired the revolver into the mattress (or the pillow). It is difficult to imagine Dean Martin either attempting or faking suicide. He liked being alone, and being left alone, which was the one thing that Frank couldn't bear.

IT WAS THE age of the nightclubs with the catchy names and the glamour. There was El Morocco, with its blue zebra-striped seat cushions, and the Stork Club on Fifty-third Street, just east of Fifth Avenue, where Grace Kelly's engagement to the Prince of Monaco was revealed in 1956. The 21 Club, with its famous receiving line of cast-iron jockeys, stored the private wine collections of celebrities ranging from John F. Kennedy and Richard Nixon to Marilyn Monroe and Frank Sinatra. At the Latin Quarter, which was founded by Lou Walters, father of Barbara, in 1942, Sinatra and Ella and the Andrews Sisters performed. French Casino was where Sugar Ray Robinson once did a soft shoe in top hat and tails, hosting a revue. When Café Society opened its doors on Sheridan Square in the West Village, the headliner was Billie Holiday. At the Three Deuces in Chicago, Roy Eldridge played his trumpet; at the Famous Door on Fifty-second Street in New York, Art Tatum played intermission piano. Sinatra and Leonard Bernstein first crossed paths at the Riobomba. Birdland was named after Bird (i.e., alto saxophonist Charlie Parker). The Five Spot, immortalized in Frank O'Hara's poem "The Day Lady Died," was where Thelonious Monk's legendary quartet went to town with John Coltrane on tenor sax in 1957. Their names are what's left of such other jazz clubs as the Embers, Royal Roost, and Bop City.

Of all the gin joints in all the world, the Copacabana reigned supreme in glitz and glamour. The Copacabana never abandoned Frank, even in the early 1950s. And the Copa Room at the Sands in Las Vegas, where Frank reigned supreme in the 1960s, was modeled precisely on the New York club.

Located at 10 East Sixtieth Street, not far from the Plaza Hotel, with a PLaza phone exchange—a precious few still know it by heart: PL8-0949—the Copacabana opened its doors for the first time on November 10, 1940. It was here that Dean Martin and Jerry Lewis made their New York debut. The duo also picked the Copa as the place to do their last show together a decade later. People went to the Copa to see and be seen, and for whoever the entertainer was. It could be Sinatra, Peggy Lee, Sammy Davis, Joe E. Lewis, Della Reese, Jimmy Durante, Buddy Hackett, Billy Eckstine, Nat Cole, Tony Bennett. It's the Copa that you see in movies like *Tootsie*, *Raging Bull*, and *Goodfellas*. Barry Manilow had a huge hit with a story song that culminates in a shooting at the Copacabana, "the hottest spot north of Havana," in 1978.

Like certain other such joints, the Copa was a front. The name on the lease belonged to one Monte Proser. Jules Podell was a puppet owner, Jack Entratter the debonair host. The real owners were the biggest gangsters in New York: Frank Costello, Albert Anastasia, and, later, Carlo Gambino and Paulie Castellano. The décor of the place was Brazilian, but the menu was famous for Chinese food of the mild Cantonese style in those pre-Szechuan, pre-Hunan days: white-meat chicken chow mein and pepper steak with bamboo shoots, water chestnuts, mushrooms, and fresh tomatoes. The Copa girls wore pink hair, sequined costumes, and fruited turbans.

Perhaps the most famous night in the history of the Copa

was May 16, 1957, when some members of the world champion New York Yankees—Mickey Mantle, Whitey Ford,
Billy Martin, Hank Bauer, Yogi Berra, Johnny Kucks, and
five of their wives—had gathered. Sammy Davis, Jr., was the
show. Hecklers taunted him. Racial slurs were in the air. Billy
Martin, who roomed with Elston Howard—the first and, as
of 1957, the only African-American to play for the Yankees—
took offense. Punches were thrown. The newspapers made
merry. And the Yankees traded Martin to Kansas City, and
the epic saga of that firecracker of a player and manager was
under way.

Sammy Davis, Jr., knew a thing or two about racial prejudice. Back in Frank's lean years, the doorman at Lindy's
had turned this colored fellow away when he came by with
drummer Buddy Rich. The same thing happened at the Copa,
where Frank was performing. Buddy talked to Frank, who
asked Sammy to call him. Sammy dialed ELdorado 5-3100 and
was told to come to the club tonight. "I'm making the reservation and you're walking in there alone." "Look, Frank, I'd
rather not." "Just be there. When something is wrong it's not
going to get right unless you fix it. I know it's lousy, Charley,
but you've got to do it." This time the maître d' said: "Right
this way, sir." A couple of friends of Frank kept Sammy company through the show. When he asked for the check, he was
told that "Mr. Sinatra has taken care of it." Backstage, Frank
put his arm around Sammy's shoulder. "You did something
good, Charley." And Sammy felt he was dancing on air, or on
the ceiling, and the whole way home, in the subway and on
the Harlem streets, "I've been to the Copa," Sammy thought,
and repeated the thought, and felt "like I'd bought a brand

new Cadillac convertible—for a hundred thousand dollars."
Ford Madox Ford pictured heaven as a café in Provence. For
Sammy it was located at 10 East Sixtieth Street.

Deals were sealed or broken at the Copa. Back in 1946, Sinatra was photographed in Havana getting off a plane carrying a
briefcase—and shaking hands with mob boss Lucky Luciano
at the Hotel Nacional. In the briefcase, he was said to have
brought $2 million in cash for the exiled Luciano. (The singer
claimed he was carrying not money but his oils and a sketch
pad—he had taken up painting.) Sinatra played a similar, if
lesser-known, role in the rise of the Jewish Homeland in 1948.
This was make-or-break time for the State of Israel. The Haga-
nah, the military wing of the Zionist cause, had its headquarters
in the building adjacent to the Copa, Hotel Fourteen. Sinatra
was performing at the club, and a stranger and he got to talking
at the bar. The stranger told him he needed to get a package
delivered to the captain of a ship full of arms earmarked for
Israel. But if I do it, the feds will arrest me. Sinatra said okay. So
the next morning the stranger walked out the front door with
a satchel—and with the feds on his heels—while out the back
door went Frank with a paper bag full of cash. He went to the
pier, sealed the deal, and watched the ship sail. The stranger
was Teddy Kollek, the future mayor of Jerusalem.

And it was also at the Copa, on April 26, 1950, that Frank's
voice quit on him. He opened his mouth but no sound came out.
This was the scariest if not the most humbling moment in Sinatra's decline and fall. Still, he was back at the Copa stage on September 21 with a song written for the occasion by Axel Stordahl
(music) and Sammy Cahn (lyrics), "Meet Me at the Copa." The
song urges everyone to stop what you're doing—even if you're

"wooing"—and come to the club. New York has many other attractions: the Empire State Building, the great art museums. And "out in Brooklyn there's a ball park and a team / But I don't care a whole lot if I never see 'em!" I'd rather be right here at the Copa with you.

Deep down, Frank Sinatra was a nightclub singer. But it is after hours, and the club is going out of business.

39

CANDOR. THIS IS Sinatra sober, measured but quite candid, on the subject of other vocalists, in a 1965 *Life* article: "For my money, Tony Bennett is the best singer in the business, the best exponent of a song. He excites me when I watch him—he moves me. Vic Damone has better pipes than anybody, but he lacks the know-how or whatever you want to call it. Take Lena Horne, for example, a beautiful lady but really a mechanical singer. She gimmicks up a song, makes it too pat."

And this is what happens when Sinatra has a couple of drinks in him:

Maxine Cheshire, society columnist for the *Washington Post*, asked Sinatra whether his alleged mob connections will embarrass his buddy Vice President Agnew as they had done the Kennedy administration. This was in January 1973, just before Nixon's second inauguration. A few days later, Frank saw the writer at an event at the Fairfax Hotel. "Get away from me, you scum," he said. "Go home and take a bath. Print that, Miss Cheshire." The more he talked, the louder he got. "You're nothing but a two-dollar cunt. C-u-n-t." And he took out two dollar bills and stuffed them in Maxine Cheshire's plastic glass.

When the incident was reported to Dolly Sinatra, Frank's mom, she said: "He overpaid."

Hollywood gossip columnist Rona Barrett had infuriated

Sinatra at the time of his divorce from Mia Farrow. Barrett wrote suggestively that Mia was seen dancing with George Jacobs, Sinatra's longtime valet (and author, with William Stadiem, of *Mr. S.*, an excellent memoir of life with his volatile boss). In *Miss Rona*, her 1972 memoir, Barrett wrote that in her "heart of hearts" she always "felt Frank Junior had staged his own kidnapping. Not for money. Not for publicity. But for the attention of his father." She also wrote that, anyone seeing Frank with daughter Nancy, would feel that "If they weren't father and daughter, they could certainly pass for lovers."

At a concert, Sinatra regaled his audience with a fierce tirade against Rona Barrett at a moment when another performer might do a little standup or a stroll down memory lane. "Congress," Sinatra said, "should give Rona Barrett's husband a medal just for waking up beside her and having to look at her. . . . She's so ugly that her mother has to tie a pork chop around her neck just to get the dog to play with her. . . . What can you say about her that hasn't already been said about—[pause]—leprosy." And more, much more than this, in the same vein.

But Frank was an equal opportunity offender, and he spoke plainly, in his native vernacular. He also had an under-standable dread of being touched or grabbed by strangers in a crowd and could react angrily when it happened. The long-time Democrat campaigned for Adlai Stevenson in 1952 and '56. At the 1956 Democratic National Convention in Chicago he sang "The Star-Spangled Banner." When House speaker Sam Rayburn of Texas grabbed him, asking whether he would also consent to sing "The Yellow Rose of Texas," Sina-tra snarled, "Get your hands off the suit, creep." That may have been one of the reasons Rayburn's fellow Texan Lyndon

Johnson treated Sinatra with contempt when he accompanied Hubert Humphrey and journalist Drew Pearson on a late-night visit with the president in May 1968. Also, LBJ detested the smug sons of bitches who idolized his predecessor, and lumped Sinatra in with that crowd. The only reason he tolerated him at all is that they both hated Bobby Kennedy.

40

BY THE END of the bobby-soxer days, the American masculine ideal was changing. Maybe that statement is always true. In Hollywood films, it used to be that the hero didn't fail if he was played by Gary Cooper, John Wayne, Errol Flynn, or Clark Gable. Even in the 1940s there were exceptions, mainly from the noir tradition. Fred MacMurray plays the sap for Barbara Stanwyck in *Double Indemnity*; Robert Mitchum falls head over heels for Jane Greer in *Out of the Past*. There was the tragic gangster hero as played by James Cagney or Humphrey Bogart. And some manly specimens had glaring weaknesses and were no less attractive for it. In Hitchcock's *Spellbound*, Gregory Peck suffers from amnesia and needs the Freudian and romantic therapy that psychoanalyst Ingrid Bergman is uniquely able to give him. Dana Andrews in *The Best Years of Our Lives* (1946) was a hero in a fighter plane but can't hold a job as a soda jerk when he returns to his home town. The ultimate disaster befalls William Holden in *Sunset Boulevard* (1950). He is a kept man, a paid consort. And though his disembodied voice guides us in the voiceover, the rest of him lies face down in a swimming pool, dead in the water.

By the early 1950s, an inchoate new ideal was beginning to take shape: the cult of the outsider, the rebel. "We thought everybody in pain was holy," writes Barbara Grizzuti Harrison, a self-described bohemian looking for "the secular equivalent of the Holy Grail" in jazz bars like the Five Spot in New York City. The "we" in that sentence is meant to stand for all the

rebels who lacked causes, particularly the females of the species. The adjectives she was looking for in the men she met
were "sensitive" and "vulnerable" and "risk-taking." "We
could accept any damned nonsense from a man provided it was
haloed by poetic *feeling*." The four men Harrison singles out
as "heroes" of this radical new antiestablishment aesthetic are
Sinatra, Brando, J. D. Salinger, and Albert Camus.

Why Sinatra? Because "he bucked the crowd, as heroes are
meant to do. He was the Outsider who fought back and made
it." And because he transformed himself not only as a Capitol
recording artist but as a film star.

In his first movies, Sinatra was the sidekick, the wingman,
the naïf compared with worldly-wise Gene Kelly. In *On the
Town*, the best of the early musicals, Frank plays Chip, the hick
from the sticks with his antiquated guidebook. In keeping with
the crooner's carefully cultivated image, Chip is scared stiff of
cab-driving Betty Garrett. She does her best to persuade him to
"Come Up to My Place," and he utters a frightened "no" as the
taxi bobs and weaves amid the traffic and the potholes.

That image changed irrevocably with *From Here to Eternity*
(1953) and *Young at Heart* (1954). The latter is particularly com-
pelling as a portrait of the hero without a halo or a coat of armor
(plus, you get to hear Sinatra and Doris Day sing). *Young at
Heart* is a musical reworking of the 1938 movie *Four Daughters*,
in which a handsome composer and his piano-playing arranger-
slash-accompanist disrupt the lives of a happy small-town
family headed by widower Claude Rains. In the original, John
Garfield plays the composer's sidekick, a loser, at war with destiny; Pauline Kael thought it was Garfield's finest performance.
In *Young at Heart*, Sinatra takes the Garfield role, except that
he doesn't die in the end. Into a fake suburban paradise Frankie

From Here to Eternity.
Mondadori / Getty Images

enters and shakes things up. The ebullient, ever optimistic Laurie (Doris Day) is supposed to connect with handsome but hollow Gig Young, the man in the gray flannel suit. She falls instead for Sinatra's character, Barney Sloan, the working-class loser with the lousy attitude. Barney is a would-be composer, and a strictly small-time lounge singer, who gets to sing Gershwin ("Someone to Watch Over Me"), Porter ("Just One of Those Things"), and Arlen ("One for My Baby") and tinges each with a noir inflection. Pauline Kael wasn't crazy about it: "In the 30s when Garfield, a rootless product of the big city and the Depression, encounters the cozy life of a small-town middle-class family it enrages him by making him feel how deprived he had been; in the 50s when Sinatra, an orphan who had never found a place for himself, expresses the same kind of chip-on-the-shoulder bitterness he seems just a sorehead and loser." Bill Zinsser, reviewing the movie for the *New York Herald Tribune*, saw things differently: "That morose face, that crooked smile, that sloppy posture, those hollow eyes—all are a pleasure to behold." The film comes as close to nihilism as can be made consistent with a happy ending: Barney survives his suicide attempt and is welcomed by Laurie's family.

The antihero aesthetic goes even deeper in Sinatra's next big dramatic role, that of Frankie Machine, who plays drums, deals cards, and shoots up in *The Man with the Golden Arm* (1955). Kael: "Frank Sinatra's performance is pure gold . . . rhythmic, tense, and instinctive, yet beautifully controlled." Sinatra was a little bummed out when Ernest Borgnine, in *Marty*, beat him out for the Oscar, but no way was Hollywood in 1955 going to favor a smack addict over a Bronx butcher who lives at home with his Italian mama and meets a nice girl, a high school teacher, at a dance.

41

SCOTT FITZGERALD WAS quite wrong about there being no second acts in American lives. We have cultivated the phenomenon of the spectacular comeback. We have a weakness for them: Apple when Steve Jobs returned to the helm; England after the blitz; Europe after the war; even, or especially, Richard Nixon, the "New Nixon," who enjoyed or endured at least two posthumous lives after pronouncing himself dead in 1962—"Gentlemen, you won't have Nixon to kick around anymore"—six years before he was elected president.

Sinatra, who arguably enjoyed the swiftest rise in entertainment history, also had (in Martha Weinman Lear's choice words) "the most fantastic comeback in show-business history, because he really *had* been reduced to total schlephood, not only professionally, which we can forgive, but in the personal image, which we usually cannot."

How bad was it when Sinatra was down and out, before he staged the fabled comeback?

He was as prematurely buried as the sister in Poe's tale "The Fall of the House of Usher."

Sammy Davis paints this word-picture of the lonely abandoned hero in *Yes I Can*: "Milton [Berle] offered me a lift but the world was beautiful and I felt like walking in it. I headed downtown, crossed 51st Street and as I passed the Capitol Theater, I thought about Frank. I'd read that he was in town and I was wondering where he was playing and how I could get in touch with him, when I looked across the street and there he was. I started to run after him and call out to him but I stopped, my arm in the air. He was slowly walking down Broadway with no hat on and his collar up—and not a soul was paying any attention to him."

Sinatra had lost everything: his audience, his marriage, his recording contract, his movie studio, even his voice. Why? Oh, there were always more reasons than one. The gangster connection. The enmity of certain powerful newspaper columnists. The sensational extramarital affair with the Hollywood starlet. Female fans who had idolized the family Sinatra (Frankie, big Nancy, little Nancy, Frankie Jr., and now Tina) began to desert the cad just as he had deserted his wife and children. When his voice failed him at the Copa on April 26, 1950, he was told that he had suffered a hemorrhage of his vocal cords—and that the only way to get better was to keep his big mouth shut.

On top of everything, the girls who used to worship the trousers that cling to him were now a few years older, and the soldiers and sailors had come home, and they were pairing off, and suddenly Frankie seemed superfluous.

"There'll Be Some Changes Made," he sang in one of his last Columbia recordings. And quickly the changes came, and were reported with customary hyperbole. *Variety* called Sinatra's performance in *From Here to Eternity* "the greatest comeback in theater history."

When Scott Fitzgerald made that remark about second acts, he failed to anticipate the hunger we have developed for redemption narratives. What Sinatra's comeback proved was that, to recapture hearts and minds once won and then dramatically lost, it is helpful sometimes to die first, if only onstage or up on the screen.

42

SOMEDAY THERE WILL be a television station exclusively devoted to *The Godfather*, if only because, as my friend Mitch Sisskind says, American men consult *The Godfather* the way rabbis consult the Talmud. Many adult American males know long stretches of the script by heart. It is full of acute insights phrased memorably; it perpetuates an ethic; it is heaped in ethnic nostalgia; it is an elegy to a certain conception of manhood and its responsibilities. It is either a devastating critique of American capitalism or it glorifies its transmogrification, and it works beautifully either way. In my own mind parts one and two of *The Godfather* saga surpass *Citizen Kane* as the most indispensable of our films, but even if your vote goes to *Vertigo* or *Grand Illusion* or *Seven Samurai,* you have to acknowledge that *The Godfather* has added to our vocabulary—and not just our film vocabulary. When considering the claim on our attention made by these movies of Francis Ford Coppola, you might also take into account that the first line uttered in part one is: "I believe in America."

The Godfather (1972) begins on the wedding day of Don Corleone's daughter, Connie. It is a Sicilian custom that the crime lord, in his function as community leader, must grant reasonable requests made by respectful supplicants on the day of his daughter's wedding. The first two visitors have their own daughters on their minds. An undertaker wants his daughter's rapists to be punished; a baker wants a work visa for the fine

Italian lad who promises to be a good son-in-law. The third on the agenda is Johnny Fontane, the singer played by Al Martino, who has just made Connie and her girlfriends swoon with his rendering of "I Have But One Love," Vic Damone's breakout hit of 1947.*

In the novel, the godfather advises the singer to go back to his wife. Johnny says he can't. Why? He has to gamble, to drink, to go out with the guys, to chase and be chased by beautiful broads. So, Vito Corleone says, cutting to the chase, you have women troubles and your voice is sick. Tell me about this Hollywood *pezzonovante* who won't let you work.

This *pezzonovante* owns the studio, Johnny explains. He just acquired the film rights to the biggest novel of the year. And there's a character who is just like me. I wouldn't even have to act. I wouldn't have to sing. It's perfect for me and I'd be big again. Maybe I'd even win an Academy Award. But he says: "No chance. No chance."

Up on the screen, the singer—"my voice is weak, it's weak"—is so full of self-pity that Don Corleone slaps him: "You can act like a man." The don ridicules him. Has he turned into "a Hollywood *finocchio* who cries like a woman?" Consiglieri Tom Hagen and even Johnny Fontane himself have to laugh at the don's mimicry. After a pep talk and some sound counsel ("I want you to eat, I want you to rest well"), the godfather promises the boy, who is after all "a good godson," that he'll get the part.†

But the contracts have been signed.

---

*Department of *Godfather* trivia: Vic Damone auditioned for the part played by Al Martino.

†*Finocchio* in Italian slang is the rough equivalent of "faggot" or "pansy."

Johnny: "Too late. They start shooting in a week."

Don Corleone: "I'm gonna make him an offer he can't refuse."

Is there a point-by-point correspondence between the fictional life of Johnny Fontane and the career of Frank Sinatra circa 1952?

Consider the evidence:

From Here to Eternity, which won the National Book Award, was the biggest novel of its year, a major bestseller for James Jones, making his career as *The Naked and the Dead* made Norman Mailer's. Both are World War II novels. Jones's is set at an army base in Pearl Harbor in the days leading up to the Japanese sneak attack of December 7, 1941.

Sinatra had that scary hemorrhage problem with his voice ("weak") in 1950.

Sinatra had left his wife, was gambling and drinking and making a sorry spectacle of himself chasing the most beautiful of all broads around the world, for Ava Gardner was on the road, shooting films on location in Europe and Africa.

The part of Private Angelo Maggio in the film adaptation of Jones's novel was perfect for Frank Sinatra. Maggio is indomitable, brash, prone to shooting his mouth off, frail, undernourished, overmatched in body but not in spirit. (As Johnny Fontane says, "I wouldn't even have to act.") When he inevitably breaks regulations, Maggio suffers at the hands of the bigoted and sadistic sergeant in charge of the stockade, Fatso Judson, who towers over him. Fatso beats Maggio mercilessly. He dies of the blows. And he gets to die in the arms of our hero, the bugler and boxer, rebel and misfit, Robert E. Lee Prewitt (Montgomery Clift), the very image of the nonconformist hero ("If a man don't go his own way, he's nothin' "), but who thinks of himself, paradoxically, as a born soldier in this man's army.

Sinatra got the role, though he wasn't the studio's first choice.

On set, Sinatra bonded with Monty Clift and with the novel's author, James Jones. They got drunk every night. Clift was asked whether he mentored Sinatra's acting. No, Clift said. Frank was a natural. It was the other way around. Frank helped Monty with "the trumpet business and marching properly."

The movie, a major box-office hit and critical success, made Sinatra big again.* In playing Maggio, a purely dramatic role requiring no singing, Sinatra went from punk heartthrob to gutsy underdog—from singing sensation to blue-collar working stiff. History says he was exempt from the draft on account of a relatively minor medical condition. This and subsequent movies say he is an enlisted man from an ethnic group that has suffered from prejudice and is eager to assert itself as proudly patriotic, proudly American.

Do not underestimate the power of the cinematic image. Ernest Borgnine, who played Fatso Judson, walked the streets of an Italian-American neighborhood in the Bronx in preparing for his Oscar-winning role in *Marty*. When a gang of young men recognized Borgnine as the son of a bitch responsible for Frank Sinatra's death on Pearl Harbor, Borgnine had some explaining to do. He let the fellows know that he and Sinatra were pals and that he himself was Italian-American. They got along

---

*"This was the movie of its year, as *On the Waterfront* was to be the next year. And not just because each swept the Academy Awards, but because these films brought new attitudes to the screen and touched a social nerve; they weren't the same kind of winner as *Ben-Hur*." Pauline Kael, *5001 Nights at the Movies* (New York: Henry Holt, 1982), p. 269.

fine after that. Ernie thought it wise not to tell them that whenever he and Sinatra exchanged letters or cards he would sign his name Fatso and Sinatra would sign his Maggio, a lifelong habit.

There are two reasons that male resistance to Sinatra turned completely around. The first is that his voice deepened. The second is that his image changed, largely because of Maggio—and because he was able to sing so convincingly of loss, failure, and despair unto death.

Sinatra won the Academy Award for best supporting actor. He signed with Capitol Records. And he scored with a song called "Young at Heart." When he sings "Fairy tales can come true, / It can happen to you," it is as if to say "Mine just did." In leaving Columbia, he freed himself from Mitch Miller, the oboist who succeeded the sympathetic Manie Sachs as head of the A&R (artists and repertoire) department at Columbia Records. The bearded boss, who went on to host the TV show *Sing Along with Mitch*, had saddled Frank with stupid novelty numbers unsuited to his talent, such as the infamous "Mama Will Bark" (1951) duet with curvaceous TV personality Dagmar, who spoke her lines robotically, punctuated by the sound of a whining dog.

In September 1953 Sinatra was overheard on the phone saying, with characteristic bravado, "Hey, I just fired Columbia." What happened was more complicated: Columbia had decided to drop him, and the feeling of good riddance was mutual. But Sinatra was loyal to his grudges. In Las Vegas, years later, when Mitch Miller offered to shake hands, the seated Sinatra, surrounded by friends, looked up and said, "Fuck off."

THE LINKAGE OF Sinatra and Marlon Brando at the top of the ticket in *Guys and Dolls* marks a confluence too rich to go unremarked, because Sinatra is to singing what Brando is to acting: a performer who doesn't just sing a song but lives it. I am not the first to say so. Pete Hamill: "He inhabited a song the way a great actor inhabits a role"—the way Brando inhabits the roles of Stanley Kowalski in *A Streetcar Named Desire*, the rebellious biker in *The Wild One*, Terry Malloy in *On the Waterfront*, and Don Corleone in *The Godfather*. "One of the writers at the time [the 1940s] said, with more than a touch of condescension, that Sinatra sang those love songs as if he believed them," Gene Lees reports. "But of course. That was the secret. And far from manifesting a callow gullibility on Sinatra's part, this was a striking advance in the art of singing."

Take "One for My Baby (and One More for the Road)," the music by Harold Arlen, the words by Johnny Mercer, as recorded by Sinatra in June 1958. It was written for Fred Astaire, who introduced the song in the movie musical *The Sky's the Limit* in 1943. Listen to Astaire do it. It's good. It's damn good. Mel Tormé lauded Astaire as a terrific jazz singer, and he wasn't kidding. Or listen to Perry Como do it, or Etta James, or even Ella on her *Harold Arlen Songbook*. Both the song's composer and lyricist recorded the song; they both sang well, and it's a special pleasure, always, to hear a songwriter sing his own tune. Arlen called it a "wandering" song, a "typical Arlen

"One for My Baby": the singer embodies the role.

tapeworm," a "tapeworm" being industry slang for any song exceeding thirty-two bars. "One for My Baby" is half again as long, at forty-eight bars.

Sinatra not only sings but acts the song. He becomes, for the next four minutes and four seconds, a guy whose girl has just left him—left him in the rain with an extra train ticket, stood up like Rick Blaine at Paris's Gare de Lyon train station in *Casablanca*, feeling as if he's just been punched in the gut. On television, Sinatra sings it in raincoat and fedora, dressed just like Bogie. He enters a bar, takes his stool, corners the bartender. It's just before three in the morning, and the place is empty except for the two of us, so set 'em up, Joe, you've got to listen to me spill my guts. This glass is going to get me through the night.

Throughout the song, the bartender is silent, "true to his code"—the perfect listener, part witness, part therapist, part priest. The song promises to tell "a story," but the details are vague. The singer never does explain exactly what happened. This is deliberate. The song can apply to any romantic postmortem. Also, how much coherence should we be expecting from a guy who's half soused?

Sinatra sings to the piano accompaniment of Bill Miller. The piano sounds distant. Otherwise there is silence, except for soft strings when the first chorus concludes, and that broken saxophone solo near the song's close. When Sinatra sings it on television, the main props he needs—besides bar, bar stool, and bartender—are a cigarette and ashtray. Without taking off his hat and coat, he takes his seat and gives Joe his order. He lights a match when beginning the line "We're drinking, my friend" but doesn't bring it to the cigarette until he gets to the "end of a brief episode," which I cite because the phrasing here—the rubato—is exemplary. The words convey that he is a friendly drunk, alternately self-pitying (lamenting a too-"brief" love affair) and self-glorifying (describing himself as a "kind of poet"). Mercer's lyric entrusts him with a dead metaphor brought violently to life, a "torch" that must be "drowned" or it may "explode." Otherwise he drifts, as a drunken man might, into sentences that come to a period but lack true closure: "Well, that's how it goes." The music is subtle enough for Sinatra to sing it as if he's having a conversation with you. He sings softly, in a way that approximates speech but remains utterly faithful to Arlen's melody. The lyrics are the words of the last man standing at the bar.

Is it a stretch to compare our experience of the song with that of the Hemingway story set in a Madrid café at closing time, "A Clean, Well-Lighted Place"? The waiters are exchanging a few words on shutting down the place. First they have to shoo out an old man who has been drinking brandy. The old man had tried to kill himself the previous week. "Why?" "He was in despair." "What about?" "Nothing." "How do you know it was nothing?" "He has plenty of money." One of the waiters is unselfconscious and goes his merry way, but the more sensitive man, the one whose mind we enter, lives in a condition of terminal religious doubt. In this famous riff, Hemingway uses the Spanish word for "nothing" to subvert the Lord's Prayer and the Hail Mary: "Our nada who art in nada, nada be thy name thy kingdom nada thy will be nada in nada as it is in nada. Give us this nada our daily nada and nada us our nada as we nada our nadas and nada us not into nada but deliver us from nada; pues nada. Hail nothing full of nothing, nothing is with thee." As a stay against confusion, a shield against the force of that "nada," the waiter has the café where he toils, which is, at least, a "clean, well-lighted place."

This song, that story, and the image of Bogart in the rain at the Gare de Lyon station—this, you might say, is what American existentialism, as a mood or an aesthetic condition, is all about.

In my favorite of several excellent studio takes, Sinatra ends "One for My Baby" by not ending it. Instead of the terminal phrase ("that long, long road"), he fractures it into fragments of farewell ("the long," "so long," "the long," "very long") trailing off into a never-ending ellipsis . . . (In the TV appearance, he sings only "the long . . . ," then walks off into the dark.) I am not sure why he changes Mercer's "dreamy and sad" to "easy and sad" as adjectives to modify "the music," but that is a query not a quibble. The crucial thing is the sensual way he stretches the "*ea*" of "easy." (Maybe his fondness for "easy" goes back to his treatment of "uneasy in my easy chair" in "It Never Entered My Mind," which he recorded three years earlier.) In 1947 he sang "One for My Baby" in B-flat ascending to D. Now, ten years later, despite the darkening of his voice, he raised it up to C and E, a whole tone higher, with the effect of accentuating the fragility of the singing. You will find the song on the 1958 album *Only the Lonely*, arrangements by Nelson Riddle. "One for My Baby" was the last song on the record and the highlight in a group of saloon songs that includes "Angel Eyes," "Good-bye," "Blues in the Night," and "Guess I'll Hang My Tears Out to Dry." But the version to get is the previously unreleased take on the three-CD set *The Capitol Years* (1990).

Only the Lonely: the clown on the album cover is a self-portrait of the singer with a pink tear flowing from a sparkling blue eye. The first time Sinatra won a Grammy, it wasn't for singing. It was for the cover design of *Only the Lonely*.

44

THOUGH HE ORDINARILY got along well with his costars, Sinatra considered Brando a rival, and each griped about the other during the shooting of *Guys and Dolls*. When Sinatra, always in a hurry, showed his impatience in a scene they had to do together, Brando would deliberately muff a line to force another take—just to get Sinatra's goat. Curiously, each invoked the deity when speaking sardonically of the other. Brando pictured Sinatra giving God hell for letting him go bald and making him wear all those toupees and hair transplants. Sinatra called Brando "Mumbles" and quipped that if Brando were ever cast as God in a picture, he would hold out for a better part. No doubt the line Sammy Cahn wrote to order for "Come Blow Your Horn"—"make like a Mister Mumbles and you're a zero"—is a swipe at Stella Adler's prize pupil. The competition between the two actors was as real as their mutual antipathy. Brando wanted to play Frankie Machine, but Sinatra got to play the heroin-addicted hero of *The Man with the Golden Arm*. Sinatra busted up the furniture in his living room in frustration and fury on learning that Brando got the part he had coveted in *On the Waterfront* (which was, to add insult to injury, filmed in Hoboken). Tina Sinatra in her memoir remembers visiting her father in his last months. They watched *Guys and Dolls*. Came the scene with the dice and the ode to lady luck. "He still can't sing," Frank said, and both of them laughed.

Brando and Sinatra had much in common. Both were drawn to roles in which they suffer bodily punishment: Brando faces the fists of the gang leader and his henchmen in the climactic scene of *On the Waterfront*; he takes an awful beating in *One-Eyed Jacks*, the western he directed. For his part, Sinatra is bandaged from top to toe in a hospital bed in two movies. A car crash is to blame in *Young at Heart*, where, though he has bested a rich suitor for the hand of cheerful Doris Day, Sinatra is a melancholy nihilist with a drinking problem. In *The Joker Is Wild*, where he plays the real-life Joe E. Lewis, hired thugs—from an Irish crime boss—have beaten him up and severed his vocal cords.

In *Manhattan* (1979), Brando and Sinatra appear on Woody Allen's exclusive list of reasons that life is worth living—along with Groucho Marx, Cézanne's apples and pears, Willie Mays, a Flaubert novel, Swedish movies, "the crabs at Sam Wo's," Louis Armstrong's "Potato Head Blues," and the second movement of Mozart's Jupiter Symphony.

It is, of course, possible that the proper comparison to make is not to Brando but to another Sinatra costar, the complicated actor who played the doomed soldier, boxer, and bugler in *From Here to Eternity*. The jazz critic and Sinatra fan Gene Lees questions the conventional wisdom that Sinatra was "merely a surrogate for the absent servicemen" during World War II: "He said for the boys what they wanted to say. He said to the girls what they wanted to hear. The body of excellent songs that had come into existence in the United States at last found a singer worthy of them. He was the best singer we had ever heard. He was one of the best singers in history. And we knew it. He was our poet laureate." In short, he "was to American song what Montgomery Clift was to American acting."

45

AS THE TITLE character in *Pal Joey* (1957), Sinatra gets to choose between Rita Hayworth and Kim Novak—between, that is, the reigning sex queens of the 1940s (Hayworth) and 1950s (Novak). When he sings "The Lady Is a Tramp" in the movie and he gets to the couplet "She's broke, / It's oke," he shrugs his shoulders wordlessly and omits the second line. Many listeners regard this version of that great standard as second only to "I've Got You under My Skin" as Sinatra's greatest up-tempo song. Not a great movie, but you get to hear Sinatra sing "I Could Write a Book," while Kim Novak delivers "My Funny Valentine" with Trudy Erwin's voice and Rita Hayworth sings "Bewitched, Bothered, and Bewildered" with the voice of Jo Ann Greer.

How's this for machismo? Sammy Cahn: "He once said to a group of us, 'Who do you think is going to walk into this room?' and he named a lady who will be one of the great luminaries of the screen as long as movies are made." The six or eight men present were skeptical. But the lady "walked in, smiled demurely, allowed Sinatra to take her hand and lead her into the bedroom."

The lady—said to have such oral expertise as to make Linda Lovelace look like an amateur—has been identified as Marlene Dietrich, who is also supposed to have called Frank "the Mercedes-Benz of men."

Sinatra and women. Dean Martin: "When Frank dies, they're gonna give his zipper to the Smithsonian." Humphrey Bogart remarked that Sinatra thought Paradise was a place filled with women and no journalists but what he didn't realize was that he'd be better off the other way around.

PRIDE. FOR THE movie version of *The Tender Trap*, Sinatra sings the title song—one of the first Van Heusen and Cahn collaborations—over the opening credits. As the credits begin, he is a speck in the distance and he comes closer and closer as he sings the song. By the time he closes, with a jubilant doo-bee-doo scat to punctuate the instrumentals, you know this guy is on top of the world. Sure enough, in the picture he is the swinging bachelor in the orange sweater to whom all the girls are attracted. He enjoys their company, their charms, and their other virtues, and would, in short, gain the *Playboy* magazine stamp of approval until life reminds him that this is the 1950s and he had better fall in love with Debbie Reynolds, to whom, at a critical point in the film, he sings the song to the relaxed jazz piano of long-time accompanist Bill Miller. *C'est magnifique.*

When Nelson Riddle did a swinging version of the song, the arrangement called for the singer to reach a high F on the word "love" in the last bars. Sammy Cahn was in the studio after Sinatra had finished a track that was fine in every particular, save that high note. Sinatra: "Did you hear how high the note is? How can you expect me to hit such a high note?" "Because you're Frank Sinatra," Cahn said with winning logic. At which the singer retreated into the booth, began the next take, tackled the high F, nailed it, sustained it, and finished the song, glowering at Cahn the whole time.

BACK IN 1943, when Sinatra played at the Waldorf, Joe E. Lewis in his own nightclub act quipped that his friend Frank "looks like an advance man for a famine." Sinatra plays Lewis in *The Joker Is Wild* (1957) and as is so often the case with Sinatra movies, the character appears to be a projection of the actor, or perhaps a mask revealing his true self.

What you need to know about this account of Joe E. Lewis's life is that he was a talented singer who was beaten up by mob muscle when he refused to knuckle under to a gangland boss. His vocal cords are cut, leaving him unable to sing. But he manages to make a comeback making people laugh by delivering brutally honest lines ("A friend in need is a pest") or mocking his own status as a world-class drunkard: "You're not drunk enough if you can still lie on the floor without hanging on."

And, before each drink: "It's post time."

In addition to "All the Way," Sinatra sings "Chicago," "I Cried for You," "If I Could Be with You" in the 1920s manner of Lewis, Al Jolson, or Sophie Tucker.

The identification of Sinatra with Joe E. Lewis suggests that he still had it in him to be the gifted but wounded rebel, independent, intransigent, with a weakness for booze and broads.

The biographical echoes hit you in the face: the wounded vocal cords. The refusal to compromise or do things any other way but his own. The proud nonconformist. But also a self-destructive streak corked up in a liquor bottle. Unlike the lush in the movie, Frank was not a hopeless drunkard, but when he did something foolish, violent, crazy, and impulsive, it was probably because he had too much bourbon in him—as when he got together with Orson Welles on election night, 1944.*

*The friendship with Welles had legs. In a scene on the yacht in *The Lady from Shanghai* (1948), you hear Rita Hayworth (then still Mrs. Orson Welles) sing "Please Don't Kiss Me" (dubbed by Anita Ellis). You also hear the song, though faintly, on the jukebox of a bar where Everett Sloan, playing Hayworth's manipulative husband, is among the men listening and commenting on the jukebox singer and his "edge." To these ears, the uncredited voice on the jukebox sounds exactly like Frank Sinatra. See Robert Miklitsch, *Siren City: Sound and Source Music in Classic American Noir* (New Brunswick: Rutgers University Press, 2011), p. 242.

48

IT'S THAT ELECTION night. Roosevelt is reelected to an un-precedented fourth term, and Sinatra feels like crowing. He is about to begin an engagement at the Wedgwood Room of the Waldorf-Astoria, where he is staying. Welles is staying there, too, and so is the conservative Hearst columnist Westbrook Pegler, who regularly attacks President Roosevelt. Pegler has derided Sinatra, and will continue to do so. He is the "New Dealing Crooner," "bugle-deaf Frankie boy," and probably a red. Welles has his own reasons for detesting the Hearst chain, the head of which does not look kindly on Welles's *Citizen Kane*. The press tycoon forbids his newspapers from running ads for the boy wonder's movie; he fulminates against the Hollywood studio system with its "immigrants" and "refugees" (read: Jews), and Hearst's hacks never fail to cast aspersions on Welles's politics and patriotism.

So Sinatra and Welles get a few drinks in them, and Frank thinks he might be up for socking Pegler on the jaw. What happened next is subject to debate. Welles says nothing happened. Sinatra says that "when it looked for sure like Roosevelt was in for his fourth term, somebody mentioned that Pegler was in the same hotel. We got to kidding about how he was probably taking Roosevelt's victory, and I said, 'Let's go down and see if he's as tough as he writes.' So we went down and knocked on his door. When nobody answered, we went away. Nobody broke in and busted up the furniture like it's been said." Pegler claims Sinatra was "shrieking drunk and kicked up such a row in the Waldorf that a house policeman was sent up to subdue him, and did."

Well, who are you going to believe?

The vendetta with Pegler lived on. Sinatra contrived to ban Pegler from the Wedgwood Room when he was performing there. Pegler retaliated by breaking the story about Sinatra's arrest in 1938 on the quaint "charge of seduction." The Hearst columnist was a bad enemy to have. If Sinatra wasn't a "pink" draft-dodger, he was a mob stooge.

49

JUST HOW SKINNY was this "mass of joints"? In 1942, while worrying constantly about whether and how to leave the Dorsey band, he barely tipped the scale at one hundred pounds. When he and Ava were parading their passions publicly, he was up to a hundred and eighteen. By 1954, when he was sitting on top of the world—Academy Award in hand, big hit with "Young at Heart"—the thirty-five-year-old star weighed 135. *Time* magazine reported that he was now "not just a mannered crooner, but a mature pro." Military records indicate he stood just under five foot eight—two to three inches shorter than he would claim.

Skinny and slight though he was, he was trigger happy with his fists, and at a nightclub or bar, or in the men's room of same, some half-pickled customer would approach and open with a jab: "I don't think you're so tough." Milton Berle told of sitting at a ringside table with Frank, Marilyn Maxwell, Louella Parsons, and Richard Conte at the Slate Brothers Club in Los Angeles, where Don Rickles was opening. Frank excused himself to go to the john. The legendarily well-endowed Uncle Milty used his trusty line: "I don't have to go, but I'll take out with you." Sure enough some tough guy walked in and picked a fight. "The only trouble with my hanging around with Frank is that I always seemed to end up in fights," Berle commented in his 1974 autobiography. "Thank God, we're both getting older, so there are less of them, but back in the 1940s and '50s his popularity and his size seemed to make him a moving target for

every would-be tough guy." There was the night Jackie Gleason opened with his band at La Vie en Rose on Manhattan's
East 54th Street, and a night at the Rio Bomba in New York in
1943, and other nights, other fights, in Miami, Palm Springs,
and at the Moulin Rouge in Hollywood. "Frank never needed
my help in a tight spot, and I would have ended up with a couple
less bumps and bruises. But I don't regret one of them. Frank's
friendship is worth it to me."

50

AT A PARTY a friend and I were having a conversation about our favorite Sinatra songs. I chose "I've Got You under My Skin" (1956) and he countered with "At Long Last Love" (1957), although he said he was tempted by "I Get a Kick Out of You" (1953), because of Sinatra's marvelous riff on the final "you," or maybe "Night and Day" (1957), which has another of those amazing Sinatra moments, when he stretches the word "through" in the phrase "and this torment won't be through / until you let me spend my life making love to you."

What do all four of these songs have in common? All were composed by Cole Porter, whose urbanity and wit made him perhaps the ideal composer for Sinatra, with Jimmy Van Heusen a close second, followed by Jule Styne, the Richard Rodgers of Rodgers & Hart, George Gershwin, Harold Arlen, Jerome Kern, and Irving Berlin. Sinatra is the exemplary interpreter of the Great American Songbook because he can shade his emotions: his joy is edged with irony and sometimes with rue, with melancholy, and sometimes something more, a heartbreak bred in the bone.

Perhaps even more important, all four songs were arranged by a former trombonist with the Dorsey band, a genius named Nelson Riddle. Riddle was one of the best things that ever happened to Sinatra. During the singer's eight years on the Capitol label, the period of his best work (1953–61), it was Riddle who defined the Sinatra sound. If you're a newcomer to Sinatra,

I recommend beginning with *The Capitol Years*, a three-CD anthology set, and then going on to these indispensable individual albums, all of them with Riddle arrangements: *Songs for Swingin' Lovers!*, *In the Wee Small Hours*, *A Swingin' Affair*, *Swing Easy*, *Nice 'n' Easy*, *Only the Lonely*, *Close to You.*

Critic Will Friedwald: "It remained for Riddle to develop both the ballad side and the swinging side of Sinatra, or rather to extend the legacies of Axel Stordahl and George Siravo (and before him, Sy Oliver). And the Sinatra-Riddle sound has since become what we think of when we think of Sinatra; the pre-Riddle period can be reduced to a prelude, the post-Riddle era to an afterthought."

Oh, yes—you wanted to know the meaning of "swing," the word that recurs so often in Sinatra's album titles? Listen to "All of Me" (music, Gerald Marks; lyrics, Seymour Simons) on *Swing Easy* (1954). This is a song Sinatra had frequently sung in the 1940s, each time experimenting a little more with the phrasing and with how he exits from the song. Here he sings the final stanza with such exuberance as to undo the actual sense of the words. Where the line as written would require him to sing, "can't you see / I'm no good without you," he sings "can't you see / I'm just a mess without you." The emphatic "mess" sounds more like a triumphant declaration of independence than like a suitor's plea. The lyrics say one thing, the delivery says another, and the style makes it cohere. That's one way swing works.

"THE RAPTURE OF *Songs for Swingin' Lovers!* and the nihilism of *Only the Lonely,* apart from being Riddle's two favorites of the twenty-one albums he arranged with Sinatra, can be safely described as the high points of the collaboration and the zeniths of the careers of both men, individually and as a team. Still, they are hardly singular pinnacles. We could point to *A Swingin' Affair, Swingin' Lovers*'s sequel, as perhaps an even more thrilling ode to sensual syncopation, while *In the Wee Small Hours* and *Close to You,* prequels to *Only the Lonely,* are in many ways no less disturbing juxtapositions of romance and anguish." (Will Friedwald, *Sinatra! The Song Is You*)

AFTER SINATRA DIED, I overheard someone say scornfully that he was overrated: "Without his voice he would have been nothing." There must be a rhetorical term for such a statement.

"SINATRA'S VOICE WENT through range changes. His sound changed. He went from the violin with Axel [Stordhal, Sinatra's primary arranger in the 1940s], the pure violin sound, to the sound underneath, the viola, with Nelson [Riddle in the 1950s]" (Sammy Cahn). "The voice itself would evolve over the years from a violin to a viola to a cello, with a rich middle register and dark bottom tones" (Pete Hamill). In the late Sinatra of the concert years, biographer Shawn Levy even hears a tuba.

Ever since I read Charles Baudelaire's poem "Correspondences" in college, I have been attracted to the idea that we wend our worldly way "through forests of symbols" and that there are secret linkages between distinct areas of experience. (Thus, from a poem of mine called "Effects of Analogy": "Bop is to analytical cubism / as John Coltrane is to Malcolm X / as Dante is to Virgil /as a tank is to a wooden horse.") To the paradigm of musical instruments, I would suggest these further correspondences:

1940s: The Voice. Violin. Ideal medium: radio. Allegorical songs: "All or Nothing at All," "Oh! Look at Me Now." "God, he looked like a star. He had the aura of a king as he sat signing autographs with a solid-gold pen" (Sammy Davis, 1944). Occupational hazards: female mass hysteria, right-wing columnists. Foibles: Lucky Luciano, hyperactive libido, whiskey, temper tantrums.

1950s: The Capitol Years. Viola. Ideal medium: long-playing record. Allegorical titles: "You Make Me Feel So Young," "Come Fly with Me," "All the Way." Analysis based on McLuhan: "hot" FS perfect for radio and the movies, disastrous on TV. Occupational hazards: the FBI, the press. Foibles: Ava Gardner, hyperactive libido, whiskey, temper tantrums.

1960s: Chairman of the Board (so dubbed by William B. Williams of WNEW). Cello. Ideal medium: nightclub act. Allegorical titles: "Fly Me to the Moon," "It Was a Very Good Year," "My Way." Major TV success: *A Man and His Music* (1966). "Only two guys are left who are not the boy next door—Cary Grant and Frank Sinatra" (Sammy Davis). Sinatra to Tony Bennett when Bennett was enduring a crisis in confidence: "Just produce. Money follows talent." Occupational hazards: the FBI, the press. Foibles: JFK, Sam Giancana, whiskey, temper tantrums.

1970s and beyond. Old Blue Eyes. Bass trombone. Ideal medium: concert hall, Madison Square Garden, Dodger Stadium, the Pyramids at Giza. Occupational hazards: an addictive need for adulation, unwillingness to get off the stage. Foibles: Ted Agnew, Nancy and Ronnie Reagan. Mottos: "Hell hath no fury like a hustler with a literary agent." "Alcohol may be man's worst enemy, but the Bible says love your enemy." "May you live to be a hundred, and may the last voice you hear be mine."

WHEN SINATRA DIED, on May 14, 1998, some of the obituaries pointed out that his voice had sold not only beer and spirits but something far more precious. How many young couples went all the way listening to "Fly Me to the Moon" or "All the Way"?

Jimmy Van Heusen and Sammy Cahn wrote "All the Way" for the 1957 movie *The Joker Is Wild*, in which Sinatra portrays comedian Joe E. Lewis. The song, which won the Academy Award, can be heard four times in the movie. The troubled performer sings it straight; he hears himself sing it on a recording; he tries to sing it, but mobsters under the direction of a spurned boss have cut his vocal cords, and he cannot do it justice; he hears it in his head, an echo of greatness, as he walks on the pavement in front of storefronts at film's end. When you hear Sinatra sing the song as though his vocal cords were irrevocably broken, it may bring tears to your eyes. This is singing that doubles as brilliant acting.

"All the Way" is from the Capitol years, 1953 to 1961, by unanimous decision Sinatra's most fruitful and artistically satisfying period. "Fly Me to the Moon" is from the swinging 1960s, when Sinatra controlled his own recording company (Reprise) and collaborated with such arrangers as Quincy Jones, Neal Hefti, Johnny Mandel, and Don Costa, in addition to old standbys Riddle, May, and Jenkins. A Bart Howard song from 1954, "Fly Me to the Moon" did not make its mark in the

American consciousness until ten years after its composition, when Sinatra sang it with the Count Basie band in a Quincy Jones arrangement. It's the lead-off song on the album titled *It Might As Well Be Swing* (1964). When Sinatra and Basie played it for the inmates of a penitentiary, even the habitual malcontents took notice. "Fly me to the moon / and let me play among the stars"—or, as he sometimes did it, "and let me sing among the stars." For obvious reasons, the Apollo astronauts dug the song. Astronaut Gene Cernan played it in *Apollo 10* while circling the moon in May 1969. Buzz Aldrin is said to have played it on a portable cassette player when he took his first steps on the moon. (Nancy Sinatra, the singer's daughter, and Quincy Jones said this happened; Aldrin said it did not.)

One of the pleasures of *Wall Street*, Oliver Stone's 1987 movie in which the Michael Douglas character glorifies greed as an economic good, is the opening panorama of Manhattan Island; with Sinatra's rendition of "Fly Me to the Moon" in the background, it conveys the masculine swagger of the moment, the vaulting ambition and drive of the young college graduates with dollar signs in their eyes. And it swings.

Both songs testify to the masculine ideal associated with the singer, an ideal that evolved considerably over time, and which contains modifying, even antithetical, elements. "All the Way" is a soaring, intimate love song; "Fly Me to the Moon," an upbeat shout for joy. The singer of "Fly Me to the Moon" is a swinger. The singer of "All the Way" is earnest, sincere, an extremist of passion and as uncompromising as he was when singing "All or Nothing at All" nearly twenty years earlier.

When Van Heusen and Cahn wrote "All the Way" for *The Joker Is Wild*, they went to Vegas to try it out on Sinatra. He told them he would hear it before breakfast—which meant four in the afternoon. Van Heusen played the melody and Cahn sang the words and Sinatra listened, and afterward all he said was "Let's eat." Cahn's agent was there. "How could he not like that song?" she asked Sammy after breakfast. "Oh, he loved it," Cahn says he replied. "How do you know?" "Because he loves them all"—and because this was his way of not showing it.

Van Heusen—the Sinatra intimate who called Frank "Your Eminence" to his face but told a girlfriend he was "the monster"—said something similar when asked why he put up with Sinatra-mania. "Because he sings my songs, that's why." Like Cahn, Van Heusen, who admitted to being "a whore for my music," was a workaholic, addicted to writing songs.

Nelson Riddle once noted that Sinatra never praised him face-to-face, but he figured he had the singer's approval for the simple reason that he kept employing him.

55

SINATRA WAS FAMOUS, or notorious, for insisting on doing his movie scenes in one take. He felt that repetition would diminish his spontaneity. First take was best take. And as he grew in fame and power, after his fabled comeback, "One-Take Charlie" would get his way more often than not, and if not, he had no hesitation about walking away. He had signed on to play Billy Bigelow in the screen adaptation of Rodgers and Hammerstein's *Carousel*, had gone up to Boothbay Harbor, Maine, where the 125-member company was working, but walked off the set the moment he learned that the film was being shot both in CinemaScope and in a wide-screen format—a process that would require at least two takes for each shot. Although we have a pretty good idea of how he would have handled the eight-minute "Soliloquy"—he recorded it with all the drama that Oscar Hammerstein packed into the lyric—we will never know what the bench scene would have sounded like if Shirley Jones had sung the duet of "If I Loved You" with Sinatra rather than Gordon MacRae.

When shooting a movie, Sinatra wanted to get every scene wrapped with the greatest dispatch. Pauline Kael asked: "Why didn't Frank Sinatra take the professional pride in his movies that he took in his recordings?" Sammy Cahn provided part of an answer: "In pictures you never have time and Sinatra never had patience." But in the recording studio, the perfectionist took over. On the twelfth of January, 1956, it took him no fewer than twenty-two takes to do Cole Porter's "I've Got You under My Skin" to his satisfaction. It is an amazing track, maybe Sinatra's greatest up-tempo song. After the playback, the musicians spontaneously stood and applauded the arranger, Nelson Riddle, and the singer. The trombonist Milt Bernhart, who improvised a swinging trombone solo during the bridge, got his share of kudos. It was a historic moment. Whenever Sinatra sang the song in concert or for a recording, he introduced variants, as was his wont, but he always used the Riddle chart, and the trombone solo got written into it.

56

SINATRA COULD PLUCK from obscurity a song that would otherwise be a historical footnote. He resuscitated "French Foreign Legion" from a Laurel and Hardy four-reeler. He breathed new life into the 1928 song "The Lonesome Road." Among my favorites of this genre is "On the Road to Mandalay," Rudyard Kipling's poem from the volume *Barrack-Room Ballads* (1892), which is usually sung with cheery British reverence by a men's chorus. Sinatra recorded it with a driving Billy May arrangement ending in a gong strike on the album *Come Fly with Me*. The Kipling family objected, as Sinatra noted when he sang it with the Red Norvo quartet touring Australia in 1959. The poem is in the public domain, so I can quote the fragment that Sinatra sings. If you know the song, this will enhance the pleasure. If you don't know it, read these Victorian-era verses and consider the challenge of capturing their spirit while translating it into the musical idiom of swing jazz, circa 1958. Note, in line two of stanza three, a "cat" where you might reasonably have expected a "man":

> By the old Moulmein Pagoda, lookin' lazy at the sea,
> There's a Burma girl a-settin', and I know she thinks o' me;
> For the wind is in the palm-trees, and the temple-bells
>   they say:
> "Come you back, you British soldier; come you back to
>   Mandalay!"

Come you back to Mandalay,
Where the old flotilla lay:
Can't you 'ear their paddles chunkin' from Rangoon to
    Mandalay?
On the road to Mandalay,
Where the flyin'-fishes play,
An' the dawn comes up like thunder outer China 'crost
    the Bay!

Ship me somewhere east of Suez where the best is like
    the worst
Where there ain't no Ten Commandments and a cat can
    raise a thirst
'Cause those crazy bells are callin' and it's there that I
    would be
By the ol' Moulmein Pagoda, lookin' lazy at the sea
    (lookin' lazy at the sea).

Come you back to Mandalay,
Where the old flotilla lay:
Can't you 'ear their paddles chunkin' from Rangoon to
    Mandalay?
On the road to Mandalay,
Where the flyin'-fishes play,
And the dawn comes up like thunder!

57

HUMPHREY BOGART WAS the center, and Sinatra a member, of the original Rat Pack. Lauren Bacall, Mrs. Bogart, came up with the moniker in June 1955 when a dozen friends rented a train to catch Noël Coward's opening night at the Desert Inn in Las Vegas. When she saw the motley crew in their cups at the casino, she said, "You look like a goddamn rat pack." When she repeated the crack at Romanoff's restaurant in Beverly Hills a few nights later, Bogart announced the formation of the Holmby Hills Rat Pack. Bacall was appointed Den Mother. Sinatra was Pack Master, Judy Garland was Vice President, and the group came up with a coat of arms (a rat gnawing on a man's hand) and a slogan ("Never rat on a rat"). The whole thing was an in-joke. Bogart, the Rat in Charge of Public Relations, told a reporter as much. The aim, he said, was "relief of boredom and the perpetuation of independence. We admire ourselves and don't care for anyone else." After Bogart's death of cancer in January 1957, Sinatra spurned Bacall, whom he had squired; but soon he energetically organized a new solar system with himself at the center, Bishop, Davis, Lawford, and Martin in the inner circle, and certain others (the actresses Angie Dickinson, Shirley MacLaine, Debbie Reynolds, the comedian Milton Berle, the singer Phyllis McGuire, the songwriters Jimmy Van Heusen and Sammy Cahn) as orbiting or wandering planets. They were also known as the Clan. "There is no such thing as a clan or pack," Sinatra explained. "It's just a bunch of millionaires with common interests who get together to have a little fun." Joey Bishop: "I'm sick and tired of hearing things about the Clan. Just because a few of us get together once a week with sheets over our heads . . ." Sammy Davis, Jr: "Would I belong to an organization known as the Clan?"

One night in Las Vegas, with a handsome future president in the audience, Sammy told the crowd, "I'm colored, Jewish, and Puerto Rican. When I move into a neighborhood, I wipe it out."

58

SINATRA SANG "High Hopes" in Frank Capra's *A Hole in the Head* (1959). He plays single dad Tony Manetta who has trouble making the payments on his rundown Miami Beach hotel but has visions of a major Florida amusement park (years before Disney World). Tony has a weakness for dames but an unsuspected resource in his son (Eddie Hodges), an assertive older brother and sister-in-law (Edward G. Robinson and Thelma Ritter), and eventually a love interest (Eleanor Parker). "High Hopes" won the Academy Award for best song, and Frank sang it sometimes surrounded by a chorus of kids with fifties haircuts, looking earnest and cute. You heard it everywhere you went in 1959.

With changes in wording, "High Hopes" became John F. Kennedy's campaign theme song in 1960. Sinatra sang the catchy tune on the radio, and Jacqueline Kennedy joined in dutifully on campaign stops with her husband and entourage. As a twelve-year-old boy caught up for the first time in the excitement of presidential politics and the prospect of change after eight years of sameness, I well remember the new lyrics Sammy Cahn fashioned: "K-E-double-N-E-D-Y, / Jack's the nation's favorite guy." Voters are exhorted to "back Jack," who's on "the right track," with his "high apple-pie-in-the-sky" aspirations. Cahn says he couldn't find a rhyme for "Kennedy"—perhaps he dismissed "threnody" as too uppity—and therefore resorted to spelling out the candidate's name.

Maybe no one outside the Kennedy family and inner circle was as excited as Frank Sinatra as January 20, 1961, approached. In his inaugural speech that day, Kennedy said that the nation was prepared to bear any burden to spread human freedom. It was a call to action, it made its appeal to the idealism of youth, and it was in its way as triumphalist an American vision as any president has articulated in an inaugural speech. It was just as well that the blinding sun prevented Robert Frost from reading "Dedication," the new work he had crafted for the occasion, which forecast "A golden age of poetry and power / Of which this noonday's the beginning hour." Eighty-five years old, Frost gave up trying to make out the words typed on the white paper. Instead he recited from memory "The Gift Outright," a vision of manifest destiny if ever there was one, and quite a stirring one: "The land was ours before we were the land's."

Sinatra was responsible for organizing the inaugural gala at the White House on the eve of the ceremony. He enlisted an elite band of performers and artists to come together for the night's entertainment. Gene Kelly flew in from Switzerland, Sidney Poitier from France, Ella Fitzgerald from Australia, Shirley MacLaine from Japan, Keely Smith and Louis Prima from Las Vegas. Two Broadway theaters went dark so that their stars could attend: Ethel Merman (*Gypsy*) and Sir Laurence Olivier and Anthony Quinn (*Becket*). Others who attended or performed were Eleanor Roosevelt, Harry Belafonte, Milton Berle, Nat King Cole, Bette Davis, Fredric March, Janet Leigh, Tony Curtis, Juliet Prowse, Alan King, Mahalia Jackson, Roger Edens, Jimmy Durante, Bill Dana.

Nelson Riddle and his orchestra played. Sinatra hired Sammy Cahn and Jimmy Van Heusen to write special lyrics ("That Old Jack Magic"). TV pros (Goodman Ace, Norman Corwin, and

AFP / Getty Images

others) wrote dialogue. Straight man Joey Bishop, the "Frown Prince" of comedy, was appointed master of ceremonies. Leonard Bernstein composed his *Fanfare for the Inauguration of John F. Kennedy*, orchestrated for four trumpets, four trombones, seven woodwinds, and more than five other instruments. He also agreed to conduct Sousa's "Stars and Stripes Forever" and Handel's "Hallelujah Chorus."

Frank and Lenny went way back. Lenny wrote "The Riobomba" for that club's opening on December 10, 1942; Sinatra performed there in 1943; Dean Martin, too. Many years later, on August 25, 1988, when Lenny, at Tanglewood, celebrated his seventieth birthday, Francis Albert, in a Reno nightclub, raised a toast in his honor. The salutation of Frank's message to the birthday boy was "Dear Genius."

Sinatra had cabled Lenny on January 12, 1961, laying out the schedule of events for the inaugural gala. He called for an all-day rehearsal on Wednesday, the eighteenth ("and you know how much I like rehearsals"). Final orchestra rehearsals were scheduled for the morning of the nineteenth; dress rehearsal at noon. "It behooves us all to put on a really slick show," Sinatra emphasized. As "for the social side of this hoe-down": "Exhibit A will be a supper party that Ambassador Kennedy is giving in honor of the entire cast immediately after our gala performance. . . . Exhibit B is the inaugural ceremony itself at noon of the twentieth and the parade which follows. . . . Exhibit C is the little wing ding dinner which I am tossing for all of us at seven thirty on the evening of the twentieth. We will all go *en masse* from this dinner to the inaugural ball at the mayflower, which is pretty dressy for boys and girls. Black tie or white tie diamond and emeralds and all that jazz. Everything is shaping up for something that we all will be remembering for a long

Escorting Jackie at the Inaugural Ball, 1961.
Bettmann / CORBIS

long time and believe you me I don't think I have ever been so excited. Love and kisses and I'll be waiting for you."

Not everyone in the "Jack Pack" was as enthusiastic as Frank. The Kennedys disinvited Sammy Davis, Jr., because he had taken up with May Britt, a Swedish actress, and the Kennedys didn't think the country was ready for interracial couples. Sammy was hurt. Dean was furious: "If Sammy can't go, I won't go."

The afternoon preceding the event was nail-chewing time for the well-known perfectionist and control freak who organized the event.

It had started to snow on the morning of the nineteenth. It snowed all day, tying up traffic, causing honored guests to arrive late. The show was supposed to start at 8:30. The president-elect and his wife arrived at 10:15. The orchestra was in place, but Bernstein got caught up in a traffic jam and didn't raise his baton until 10:35. "That's God reminding Frank Sinatra that he's still around," Sammy Cahn said.

At the gala, Ella sang for five minutes. Gene Kelly danced. Jimmy Durante sang "September Song." Ethel Merman belted out "Everything's Coming Up Roses." Bette Davis read from a Norman Corwin radio script. Fredric March recited the speech Abraham Lincoln gave from the back of the train taking him from Washington to Springfield. Frank sang "You Make Me Feel So Young" in addition to "That Old Jack Magic" and did a comic skit with Milton Berle, making sport of NBC news anchors Chet Huntley and David Brinkley. It was nearly one-thirty in the morning when the show ended.

The gala raised, in one evening, $1.5 million toward the $4 million deficit the Democratic Party had run going back to the Stevenson campaign of 1956. "I know we're all indebted to a great friend—Frank Sinatra," the president-elect said after the finale.

"Tonight we saw excellence," said JFK.

After the ball, Frank went back to the West Coast, where he kept a "Kennedy Room" filled with mementos. Kitty Kelley: "Frank sent the President every one of his albums, plus tapes of Rat Pack hijinks in Las Vegas. In return, President Kennedy sent him a thank-you note on White House stationery; that, too, was framed and hung in the Kennedy Room."*

---

*Kennedy memorabilia was not the only thing FS collected. All his life he assiduously collected model trains. A guest house in his desert compound in Rancho Mirage, California, is consecrated to this collection. A plaque on the wall announces: "He who dies with the most toys wins."

59

THE FIVE ONSTAGE members of the Rat Pack were two Italian-Americans, one African-American Jew, one patrician Englishman, and one American Jew. The American male in all his ethnic and religious diversity was at center stage. Max Rudin on the Rat Pack nightclub act: "The vaudeville tradition that was the distant ancestor of their routines had relied on ethnic stereotypes: Irish and blacks, Germans and Jews, Italians and Poles—but as victims, as the lower-class butt of jokes. This was something altogether different, stars at the pinnacle of American entertainment who acted as if style and class and success were not at all incompatible with ethnic identification, whose art in fact proclaimed that they were truly American *because* they were Italian, or black, or Jewish.

"It was as if that mixed-race gang of street kids from *The House I Live In* had learned the lesson about tolerance and grown up to embody it. Or, better, as if the World War II platoon of countless movies—Kowalski, Bernstein, Johnson, Maggio— had moved to Vegas; having beaten the Nazis, they would now conquer America."

Sinatra, Martin, and Davis made fun of themselves, their backgrounds, their attitudes, their ethnic identities. It was one way of showing indifference to the taboos they were busting.

When Sammy lost an eye in a car accident, both Sinatra and Martin wore eye patches in solidarity.

At a bash for Sinatra's forty-second birthday at Hollywood's

Gab Archive / Getty Images

Villa Capri in 1957, Dean sang "He's the Wop" to the tune of Cole Porter's "You're the Top." Deana Martin, Dean's daughter, tells us "they would continue to bat different versions of that song back and forth at each other over the years."

The original Vegas gig that grew into "the Summit at the Sands" was Dean's—he had contracted to do twice-yearly, six-week bookings for five years in the Sands' Copa Room. As audience members, Frank and Sammy felt free to crack wise. Pretty soon the casino's flashing neon sign was amended from "PRE-SENTS DEAN MARTIN" to add "MAYBE FRANK, MAYBE SAMMY." One night in 1959 Sinatra joined Martin onstage. Frank said Dean had a suntan "because he found a bar with a skylight" and Dean debunked the maxim that carrots are good for your eyes: "I stuck one in mine last night and it hurt."

Bishop (born Joseph Gottlieb) to Sinatra and Martin: "I got my own group, the Matzia." (When the word is accented on the second syllable, it is Yiddish for "a bargain.") Martin to Davis: "I'll go to *shul* with you, but don't touch me." Davis: "How do you like standing in the back of the bus, Dean?"

They called Sammy Davis "Smokey." Martin advised Sammy against drinking water. "That stuff'll make you rust."

By present-day standards, their antics sometimes crossed the line of bad taste, or bad judgment—as when Dean Martin lifted Sammy Davis (barely five feet three) in his arms and thanked the NAACP for this "trophy." At the time, this kind of humor qualified as a brand of "wild iconoclasm" and "a devil-may-care nonconformity," as Robert Lagare wrote in the June 1960 issue of *Playboy*. I would argue further that the Rat Pack antics amounted to a critique of racism and bigotry, debunking these things by turning them into jests. What would sound like a slur in some contexts ("dago" as a synonym for "pally") became in-jokes for the sophisticated. Do not forget that Sinatra, who had stood up for black musicians as far back as the Dorsey days, had a long and proud record of championing the rights of African-American and Jewish musicians and entertainers.

Martin made a living off the notion that he was a lazy drunkard. When the Rat Pack was the Jack Pack, Dean said he was a candidate for the position of "Secretary of Liquor" if JFK won the election. That was the image he cultivated, and whether it is only somewhat more factual than other comic routines (such as Jack Benny's professed stinginess and vanity), Dean certainly preferred golf and playing cards to the sort of confrontations that drew Sinatra as iron filings to a magnet.

Sinatra and Davis, on the other hand, burned with ambition and pushed hard for pushing hard. You can make it here if you give it your best shot. Only in America, land of the dream. Upward mobility, baby.

Sammy Davis called his autobiography *Yes I Can*.

In the title song of *Come Blow Your Horn*, Sinatra gives you—in a Sammy Cahn rhyme—"the whole megillah in a one-word speech: Reach."

60

THE RAT PACK crew filmed *Ocean's Eleven* during the day, entertained the customers at the Sands at night, and still had time to play. Mythologized or not, this was Sinatra at the height of his glory. He was at the center of a bunch of cool, well-connected cats who had their own "ring-a-ding-ding" lingo that was heavy on "birds" and "clydes" and punctuated with iterations of the verb "to dig." They enjoyed their smokes and their hours wrapped in towels in the most exclusive steam room in the state of Nevada, and they dug the idea of being a bunch of war heroes who have one last caper in them. Dean's robe had the word "Dag," short for "Il Dago," embroidered on the left breast pocket. Frank's robe had "Leader" in that spot. Sammy's was brown and said "Smokey." When Kirk Douglas visited the Sands, Frank and Dean insisted he make use of the sauna. He went, took off his clothes, and entered the steam room. In the mist, he could see a naked woman, beautiful and friendly, sitting next to him.

Sinatra and team called their nightclub act the "Summit at the Sands," and the announcements ahead of time gladdened the hearts of Las Vegas casino owners as people rushed to book rooms and suddenly you couldn't easily score a reservation at the Sands or anywhere nearby.* They called it the "Summit,"

*"Although February was traditionally a slow month [for the Sands], the hotel received eighteen thousand reservation requests for its two hundred

because of the currency of the word, as face-to-face meet-
ings between heads of state Eisenhower and Khrushchev were
planned and publicized. The grandeur of the term suited the
singer. It was a summit of performers who enjoyed their own
company, and, as one of Dean Martin's too-drunk-to-care jokes
had it: How did all the rest of these people (that is, the audience)
get into their hotel room?

The guys denied they were a "clan," but with a wink.
"You're looking prosperous, pally," Frank might say, and Dean
would reply, "Clean liquor." The booze and the womanizing
are the stuff of legends. And yet, allowing for the inevitable ex-
aggeration, everything you've read about the "Summit at the
Sands" is probably true. There were girls galore, and the guys
who came to the party included assorted Mafiosi as well as the
junior senator from Massachusetts who was running for president. Peter Lawford, of the inner circle, was, after all, John F.
Kennedy's brother-in-law. He and Frank went all the way back
to *It Happened in Brooklyn*, in which Peter had played the heir
of a dukedom. Now, as Pat Kennedy's husband, he was one step
away from American royalty: "Peter-in-Lawford," as Frank
called him (with typical subtlety), or "Brother-in-Lawford."
When JFK visited the Sands, he was treated the way Moe Green
wanted to treat Michael Corleone in *The Godfather*: "The chef
cooked for you special, the dancers will kick your tongue out,
and your credit is good. Draw chips for everyone in the room so
they can play on the house."

rooms." Max Rudin, "Fly Me to the Moon: Reflections on the Rat Pack," in
American Heritage, December 1998, p. 55.

61

IN JAMES WOLCOTT'S formulation, Sinatra "triangulated" Hollywood (the orgiastic Rat Pack scene, the agonizing later years of Marilyn Monroe), Washington (the brothers Kennedy), and the Mafia. After helping to get JFK elected in 1960, Chicago mob boss Sam Giancana, a.k.a. Momo (or Mooney), felt betrayed when Bobby Kennedy's Justice Department went after him with no mercy. Perhaps it is the fate of any eternal triangle that each of the three parts ends up mad as hell at the others.

Recollecting the 1950s and sixties, Peter Lawford, the British-born actor who had married President Kennedy's sister, admitted that he "was Frank's pimp and Frank was Jack's. It sounds terrible now, but then it was really a lot of fun."

Among their crowd, the sex those days was more casual and more frequent than the public realized. Marilyn, who spent a fair amount of time at Frank's compound in her last sad summer, had had hot affairs with both the president and the attorney general. These may well have been contributing factors to her depression and instability and finally her fatal overdose. Another one of JFK's preferred bedmates, whom he met at the Sands, was Judith Campbell, who was also a Giancana moll. When J. Edgar Hoover found out about the double connection, that put the kibosh on the Campbell affair. Suddenly the Kennedys wanted nothing to do with Sinatra.

The drama came to a head in March 1962. The president had accepted an invitation to visit the Sinatra compound in Palm

Springs for a few precious days and nights. Never one to settle for half measures, Sinatra built a whole new wing to his compound in preparation for the presidential visit. He added cottages for Secret Service agents, installed extra phone lines, a switchboard, and teletype facilities. He constructed a heliport for the presidential helicopter and a flagpole modeled on one he saw at the Kennedy compound in Hyannis Port, Massachusetts.

Suddenly, though, none of it mattered. All of Sinatra's campaigning for Kennedy, the entertainment he organized for the Inaugural Ball, was forgotten. Now Sinatra meant Mafia, and all that "chicky boy" lingo was strictly Pastville. Bobby Kennedy called Peter Lawford to relay the message that JFK wouldn't be staying with Frank as planned after all. But the Kennedys weren't canceling Palm Springs altogether: the president and entourage would be spending the weekend as the guest of Bing Crosby, Sinatra's chief rival—and a Republican to boot.

How did Sinatra react to the snub? How do you think? He took a sledgehammer to the heliport, cursed and swore at Bobby, cut messenger-boy Lawford out of his life for-fucking-ever, and never forgot. The role that was meant for Lawford in *Robin and the Seven Hoods* went instead to Bing Crosby.

62

IT WAS IN 1954—November 5, to be precise—that Frank helped Joe DiMaggio break and enter Marilyn Monroe's apartment. Except that it wasn't her apartment. Their little adventure came to be known as the "Wrong-Door Raid." The two men were having dinner with friends at the Villa Capri in Hollywood one night when they excused themselves and left together in a car. One of the men carried a flash camera. Joe's marriage to Marilyn had hit the rocks. She wanted a divorce. He wanted to know if she was seeing someone else. There were rumors of a lesbian attachment. A detective had turned something up, so the two most famous Italian-Americans of their time drove to a West Hollywood apartment they thought was occupied by the blond goddess and her phantom beau or belle. They kicked in the door, but the terrified woman in her nightgown inside was a mere mortal named Florence Kotz, a secretary by occupation, who eventually brought suit and settled out of court for $7,500. The building's landlady reported witnessing the two men in heated conversation outside. Sinatra was animated, smiling, "jumping up and down." DiMaggio was just furious. After the story was written up in *Confidential* magazine, DiMaggio, who disliked publicity and hated breaches of decorum, cooled on Sinatra. From that time on, the two seldom spoke.

There is a 1949 photograph of the two of them in the dugout, DiMaggio in Yankee pinstripes, Sinatra in a natty suit with peaked lapels, both of them smiling. But in retrospect, a clash between the two titans was inevitable. The two men dominate any discussion of Italian-Americans in the modern era. Each represented success as well as successful assimilation. Each was at the height of his glamorous profession, and each conducted himself in a distinctive way. But the two men also embodied contrasting ideas of masculinity. Frank was in-your-face, loud, a magnet for journalists and gossip columnists. Joe was just as intense, but a lot more private. There were other ballplayers— Ted Williams, for example—with more impressive numbers. But Joe was the hero, the outfielder who made the hard catch look easy, the batter who got the clutch hit that won the game. His fifty-six-game hitting streak in 1941—widely considered to be the one unbreakable baseball record in the books— punctuates Robert Mitchum's narrative in the 1975 film adaptation of Raymond Chandler's *Farewell, My Lovely*. Mitchum keeps up with the streak, game by game, rooting for Joe and the Yankees. Hemingway idealized DiMaggio in *The Old Man and the Sea*. The "great DiMaggio" is an inspiration to Santiago, the fisherman, because Joe shows grace under pressure, plays when injured, plays uncomplainingly. "I must have the confidence and I must be worthy of the great DiMaggio who does all things perfectly even with the pain of the bone spur in his heel." Santiago doesn't know what a "bone spur" is, but he is reasonably certain that, bone spur or not, "the great DiMaggio would stay with a fish as long as I will stay with this one."

Though totally different in style and temperament, the graceful, reticent, dignified DiMaggio and the hotheaded, pugnacious, assertive Sinatra were genuine American heroes at a moment of crisis for Italian-Americans. After all, we were at war with Italy, one of the Axis powers—a minor power, to be sure, but an enemy all the same. Mussolini was not, or not merely, a figure of fun, a pompous dictator who made the disastrous decision to throw all in with Hitler instead of maintaining a cordial distance, as the equally Fascist Franco did in Spain. Our most lasting image of Mussolini may be the sight of him and his mistress hanging upside down after being executed by partisans. But until Mussolini fell, Italy was allied with Nazi Germany, and a fair amount of suspicion attached itself to Italian-Americans, who had gone from being victims of one kind of caricature—the greenhorn with the strong accent, the bootlegger with the machine gun—to another: the urban hoodlum at home, a dems-and-dose alien in our midst, even if a less formidable enemy abroad than Germany or Japan. President Roosevelt disparaged Italians as "opera singers," and ordered five thousand Italian-Americans to be rounded up and sent to internment centers. One of them, held at Ellis Island for three months, was in fact the opera singer Ezio Pinza, who would go on to sing "Some Enchanted Evening" and "This Nearly Was Mine" on Broadway in Rodgers and Hammerstein's *South Pacific* after the war was over. At such a time, what glamour boys DiMaggio and Sinatra did in their respective fields of endeavor was invaluable to compatriots of Italian descent.

When, in 1958, the Italian ambassador announced that Frank Sinatra had been named the Italian-American Man of the Year, Joe was on hand to bestow the "Star of Italian Solidarity" on his erstwhile buddy. But the friendship turned sour for good when Sinatra and Monroe had their inevitable affair and she became a regular at Sinatra headquarters in Palm Springs where there were always extra rooms with their own bathrooms and everything was deluxe. For details, read Kitty Kelley's book: "The friendship between Joe and Frank ended when Sinatra started dating Marilyn and passing her around to his friends. Joe never

forgave Sinatra or Peter Lawford for allowing Marilyn's affair
with Robert Kennedy to take place. He was bitter about them
after her suicide and barred both men from attending her funeral in 1962."

That's one version. Whatever the cause, Marilyn was taking
a lot of pills in those last days and would allegedly walk around
the place naked, opening doors and walking right into crowded
rooms. Shawn Levy, from whose 1998 book *Rat Pack Confi-
dential* I take this last piece of information, says justly of Miss
Monroe: "Flaubert would've based his entire career on her."
She was a mess: too much booze, too many pills. Her death
in August 1962—whether an accident or something worse—
implicated powerful men: she had had affairs with both John
and Robert Kennedy as well as with Sinatra and who knows
who else in that sex-happy, testosterone-charged circle. It is
said that the affair with RFK had the real sizzle. One question
that gets asked is: How ruthlessly self-protective was Bobby
Kennedy? Says Levy: "She was the one true sign before Dallas
that something was extremely rotten in their world."

LIKE THE SINGER, perhaps more so, the junior senator from Massachusetts suffered from an acute case of satyriasis. He liked partying in the Las Vegas casino where there were "blow jobs on the house." Following one of his performances at the Sands, Sinatra introduced candidate John F. Kennedy to Judith Campbell. It happened during the filming of *Ocean's Eleven*. Sinatra arranged a room-service lunch for Kennedy and Campbell in his private suite, and thus began a secret, torrid two-year affair that continued after Kennedy occupied the White House and despite the president's awareness that Campbell was sleeping not only with him but with Sam Giancana, head of the Chicago mob. All this we know from the FBI files that Sinatra obtained in 1981 under the Freedom of Information Act and which were edited for book publication under the title *The Sinatra Files: The Secret FBI Dossier* (2000) by journalists Tom and Phil Kuntz. According to Giancana's brother and son, "Frank reported to Mooney [i.e., Giancana] that Jack was immediately taken by this woman who reminded people of his wife, Jackie." Giancana was reportedly close to ecstatic. He would adopt her as a moll. It would all work out to his advantage even if the dashing new president reneged on his father's word.

GIANCANA AND HIS associates thought they had a line into the White House. Old Joe Kennedy was a bootlegger who understood how things work. In 1960, Kennedy needed all the help he could get. The deal was, the Teamsters would deliver West Virginia—a poor, heavily Protestant state with a strong anti-Catholic bias—in the May 10th primary against Hubert Humphrey. It was going to cost them half a million, but they would do it. Then Chicago, Giancana's home turf, would put Illinois over the top in the general against Nixon. The quid pro quo did not have to be spelled out. It was understood that, in exchange for such election-year favors, the Kennedy administration would go easy on mob activities. Besides, hadn't Giancana saved old Joe's life? Frank Costello was going to put out a contract on Joseph Kennedy and Sam talked him out of it. Joe promised Giancana the moon: if you help us elect him president, my boy "won't refuse you, ever."

None of them had reckoned on Robert F. Kennedy's righteous moral indignation, which took the form of the attorney general's holy crusade against organized crime. Bobby had already incurred Sam Giancana's eternal hatred when, before the McClellan Committee hearings in 1959, the Mafia boss took the Fifth and laughed a little nervously at the persistent questioner. Bobby said, "Are you going to tell us anything or just giggle?" then taunted: "I thought only little girls giggled." A smile froze on Giancana's face. A smile that said *You're going to die*. Giancana was "thinkin' about a night with his brother at the Cal-Neva [resort at Lake Tahoe]. It was all so funny . . . I couldn't help it. What a bunch of fuckin' hypocrites."

When Joseph Kennedy suffered a debilitating stroke, it removed one buffer in the chain. But was it really possible that Jack and Bobby didn't know what their dad had done to get Jack elected president, and what debts he had incurred?

Besides hating the Brothers Kennedy, Giancana was furious with Sinatra (whom he dubbed "the canary") for failing to exercise his supposed influence with the young president. He was supposed to act as a conduit, for crying out loud. Federal wiretaps caught a conversation between Giancana and Johnny Formosa, a henchman. "Let's hit Sinatra," Formosa said. "Or I could whack out a couple of those other guys, Lawford and that [Dean] Martin, and I could take the nigger [Sammy Davis, Jr.] and put his other eye out." Giancana said, "No, I've got other plans for them." They were all assholes and prima donnas, these show-biz types. But they made good bagmen. And Sinatra? "I guess I like the guy," Giancana said. "Shit, it's not his fault that the Kennedys are assholes. But if I didn't like him, you can be goddamned sure he'd be a dead man." It's been said that Giancana decided against whacking the canary because he wanted to hear him sing "Chicago" one more time.

65

THE KIDNAPPING OF Sinatra's son just two weeks after the assassination of JFK was the work of amateurs. Sinatra paid the ransom, and followed the elaborate instructions for delivering it. Because the kidnappers demanded that he phone them from phone booths exclusively, he started carrying a roll of dimes in his pocket at all times—a habit he never broke.

Frank Jr. was released on December 11, 1963, the day before his pop's forty-eighth birthday. The three felons who snatched the boy, then nineteen, were arrested and swiftly brought to trial. Most of the ransom money was recovered, and Frank Jr. did not seem the worse for wear. In court, the kidnappers' defense rested on the contention that the kidnapping was a hoax, a publicity stunt staged by Frank Jr. Frank Sr.'s terse comment: "This family needs publicity like it needs peritonitis." But the fact that the incident happened so soon after November 22 aroused the notice of numerous newspaper columnists then, and continues to interest conspiracy theorists who suspect mob involvement in the death of the president. I do not, incidentally, use the term "conspiracy theorists" with the intent to deprecate their efforts. The category of those who doubt that Kennedy was killed by a lone gunman includes two presidents, J. Edgar Hoover, a Warren Commission member, many Kennedy associates, the presidential physician, the mayor of Chicago, the producer of *60 Minutes*, and Frank Sinatra.*

At the time of the kidnapping, Frank Jr. was touring as part of a Tommy Dorsey nostalgia package that included a chorus group modeled on the old Pied Pipers as well as the "voice of the name bands," Helen Forrest, who had sung with Artie Shaw ("All the Things You Are"), Benny Goodman ("Taking a Chance on Love"), and Harry James ("I Had the Craziest Dream"). Back in 1943, Helen had topped a *Down Beat* magazine poll as the nation's favorite female vocalist—ahead of a formidable list that included runners-up Helen O'Connell and Anita O'Day, not to mention Peggy Lee, Jo Stafford, Dinah Shore, Billie Holiday, Marion Hutton, Mildred Bailey, Lena Horne, and Ella Fitzgerald. (On the male side, the top three were Sinatra, Crosby, and Bob Eberly, O'Connell's counterpart in the Jimmy Dorsey Orchestra.) When she sang with Sinatra's nineteen-year-old son in 1963, Forrest stole the show. "She never sang with Dorsey, but she sang with the best and is the best," wrote a Canadian reviewer. "Oh, yes, Frank Sinatra, Jr., also sang," the scribe added. On the occasion of Frank Jr.'s New York café debut, the writer for *Billboard* opined that Miss Forrest remains a "wow of a performer," but that the younger

---

*Under the heading "J.F.K.," the *New York Times Book Review* of June 17, 2007, printed a letter by Norman Mailer and three other signatories who professed themselves outraged by a book review maintaining that conspiracy theorists should be "ridiculed, even shunned . . . marginalized the way we've marginalized smokers." Among others identified in the letter as believing that President Kennedy was killed as the result of a conspiracy are "John Kennedy's widow, Jackie," his brother Bobby, two members of the Senate Intelligence Committee, seven of the eight congressmen on the House Assassinations Committee and its chief counsel, and the Secret Service agent who rode with the president in the fateful limousine.

Sinatra "sings like, sounds like, and gestures like his father, almost to the point where it's unfortunate."

Well, maybe they're right, those commentators who say he should have pursued a different line of work. But maybe it is inevitable that he didn't. In any event, the claim that the young man staged his own kidnapping for whatever complicated reason is a legal maneuver that becomes a calumny when repeated. As if having the name Frank Sinatra, Jr., wasn't burden enough, he needed this ordeal and these rumors, too.

66

ON A VISIT to Mount Holyoke College in 1992 I was invited to tea by Brad Leithauser and Mary Jo Salter, poets then on the faculty there, and discovered they are big Sinatra fans. Brad played the *Swing Easy* and *Songs for Young Lovers* albums. He took a special delight in Sinatra's handling of Ira Gershwin's lyric in "A Foggy Day (in London Town)," especially his unexpected staccato five-fold iteration of "shining" in the verse, "And in foggy London town, the sun was shining (shining shining shining shining) everywhere."

All fans have their favorites.

Harry Connick, Jr., singles out the moment "When he sings 'no' eleven times in 'Mood Indigo,' or stretches 'e-e-ev-vr-ery" in 'I Love Paris.'"

The poet Molly Arden opts for "lovely," in "Weather-wise, it's such a lo-o-ovely day" (from "Come Fly with Me") as an example of "how he bends a note to make the word come to life."

My own favorite Sinatra moments:

- Jerome Kern's "They Didn't Believe Me" in front of a live 1940s audience, with the last line of the song repeated with a flourish.
- The time he sang "Let It Snow, Let It Snow, Let It Snow" (Styne and Cahn), in a slow tempo, with only a piano accompaniment, as if it were an intimate ballad.

- The word "weird" stretched into two syllables, with the accent on the second, in the phrase "singing weird melodies" in "The Birth of the Blues," one of his last Columbia recordings.
- "So goodbye, farewell, ta ta, and also Amen" when the line as written is "So goodbye, dear, and Amen" in Cole Porter's "Just One of Those Things" (in concert).
- The bridge in waltz time on the second go-round in Rodgers and Hart's "My Funny Valentine" (*Songs for Young Lovers*).
- "A-a-a-ages ago, last night" in Harold Arlen's "Last Night When We Were Young" (*In the Wee Small Hours*).
- The "you" in "each time I do / just the thought of you" in Porter's "I've Got You under My Skin," and the tails (or codas) of "Too Marvelous for Words" (high) and "How About You?" (low), all on *Songs for Swingin' Lovers*.
- The cheerful chauvinism in "It's Nice to Go Trav'ling" (Van Heusen and Cahn), where we snap our fingers as the cheerful traveler and bon vivant confides that the girls in exotic lands are all very well and good, but they "just don't have / what the models have on Madison Ave" (*Come Fly with Me*).

On a trip to visit my mother in Florida, my wife, Stacey, and I watched *Stalag 17* starring William Holden. In the movie, set in a German POW camp in a dismal December during World War II, the guys have a little makeshift party one night, and one of them plays guitar and sings "I Love You," an old 1920s tune by Harlan Thompson (music) and Harry Archer (lyrics). I liked the melody, and when we flew home to New York, I looked to see if Sinatra had recorded it. Yes, in one of his first Capitol recording sessions with Nelson Riddle, in 1953. The moment of listening to it for the first time is dear to me, because of the sublime difference between the movie's catchy tune and Sinatra's treatment of it. It is the simplest possible lyric, consisting mostly of reiterations of the title phrase. But each time Sinatra sings (or speaks) the phrase it sounds different. And Nelson Riddle brings in the brass to punctuate with exclamation points. The song ends with Sinatra's patented caressing of the second-person-singular pronoun when he pleads with his girl for "the words that make *you* mine."

In a 1999 issue of the magazine *Callaloo*, Reuben Jackson, archivist of the Smithsonian's Duke Ellington and Ella Fitzgerald collections, published his obituary poem "Frank," which begins:

> *like god*
> *or miles,*
> *no second name is*
> *needed.*

Jackson picks out "In the Wee Small Hours of the Morning," the title cut on the album of the same name, for "its longing / unpretentious / and haunting as / moonlight." He also characterizes the song as "a 32 bar ashram."

I asked several friends whom I knew to be jazz buffs to pick a favorite Sinatra moment and comment on it. "I love Sinatra," the essayist Phillip Lopate writes, "and what springs to mind is his version of 'It Never Entered My Mind,' where he makes the most of the great lyrics, largely because his voice is best at rue and regret. When he sings 'Now I even have to scratch my back myself,' there's a nice touch of humor in the way his voice rises to suggest the awkwardness of the situation. His maudlinness is under control, it's a very balanced and sane expression of all we take for granted and then lose."

The jazz singer Annette Sanders relates: "There was a special moment with Frank in the room. I was singing with a vocal jazz group opening for Sammy Davis in Atlantic City and we were asked to sing at a Liza Minnelli after-hours birthday party. We sang 'Spring Is Here' *a capella* and the line 'maybe it's because nobody loves me' really got to Frank. He couldn't stop crying. I'll never forget it."

The composer and poet Lera Auerbach grew up in Chelyabinsk, an industrial city at the gateway of Siberia. The Chelyabinsk province, said to be the center of Soviet nuclear research, was closed to all foreigners until 1992. "Somehow my parents acquired a Sinatra record," she writes in "Listening to Sinatra in Siberia." Sinatra's songs were "magic spells" for the family. "I asked my cousin, who knew a little English, to translate them. The lines about facing all, standing tall, and doing it 'my way' resonated with me. In a world of uniforms and grayness, pioneers' red neck-scarves and long meaningless Communist-party speeches, where I was expected to follow others, to share their beliefs, to do only what's allowed, Sinatra's words became a personal manifesto, an inner spell to ward off the outside. 'My Way' gave me courage and strength. 'I will do it my way,' I would repeat to myself during some of the most crucial moments of my life. The phrase was a calling; I recognized it and followed its voice, leaving my homeland behind."

The poet Michael Burkard speaks of the moment in "I Get a Kick Out of You" "where in the second verse when he says 'terrifically' he prolongs the iffffff and sounds like he is snifffffffing cocaine (even though he is sure it would bore him 'terrifically too')."

Former U.S. Poet Laureate Billy Collins, whose poems are filled with references to jazz musicians: "I like the way he and only he says 'chick' and 'dame.' "

The dance critic Mindy Aloff singles out the 1958 recording of "One for My Baby (and One More for the Road)," which "remains as fresh as the first Lucky Strike from a brand-new pack, and it still plays freely on my inner juke box. It's one cover Sinatra made of an Astaire original where Sinatra's version makes the song more interesting. Every phrase is alive and different from every other phrase—yet the effect is of simple, bedrock expression, Denby's 'speech in the silence of the night.'* The warm and slightly delaying tenderness with which Sinatra's singing voice twice embraces the word 'baby' in the title and the touch of a shuddering chill that follows in his utterance of 'and one more for the road,' where one can't quite tell (at least I can't) if the sound is song becoming speech or speech struggling to hang onto song, are probably my favorite moments— although Riddle's astounding addition at one point of what sounds like soft strings as momentary comfort to Bill Miller's impeccably suave roadhouse piano, and the jawdropping surprise of a pure, late cry from a reed instrument (played by Gus Bivona?), are pretty traffic-stopping also. Trumpeter, arranger, and conductor Billy May is also listed on the credits, but I don't know in what capacity. . . . The feeling of the Sinatra-Riddle-Miller-Bivona-May take is of retrospection beyond brokenheartedness, which thins into air.

---

*The reference is to the poet and dance critic Edwin Denby.

"I looked up the circumstances for this recording in something called *The Mojo Collection* (4th ed.). The entry, unsigned, notes that at first Sinatra worked solely with Miller on the ivories. He returned the next day for a second try. He said, 'Word had somehow got around, there were 60 or 70 people there, Capitol employees and their friends, people off the street, anyone. We had kept this song to the last track of the session. Dave Cavanaugh knew how I sang it in the clubs and he switched out all the lights bar the spot on me. The atmosphere in that studio was exactly like a club. Dave said 'Roll 'em.' There was one take and that was that. The only time I've known it to happen like that."

Lloyd Schwartz, who won a Pulitzer Prize for his music criticism in 1994, seconds the motion: "One of Sinatra's greatest performances is his now-famous 'unreleased' 1958 version of 'One for My Baby' (ultimately issued in 1990 on *The Capitol Years*). Instead of the expected, conclusive 'that long, long road,' he trails off—with heartbreaking resignation—singing 'the long . . . that long . . . it's long . . .' "

Schwartz adds: "Rodgers & Hart's 'It Never Entered My Mind' (*In the Wee Small Hours*, Capitol, 1955, arranged and conducted by Nelson Riddle) was a song waiting for Sinatra. As in most of Lorenz Hart's lyrics, the subject is really language itself—how turns of phrases mirror the inevitable, if unexpected, and mostly unwelcome, twists our lives take." Schwartz quotes the stanza beginning "Once I laughed." The singer recalls when he heard his lover "saying" that there would come a time when he'd "be playing solitaire, / uneasy in [his] easy chair." Lloyd Schwartz's analysis:

" 'Once.' Sinatra's voice carries the narrative wonder of 'once upon a time,' only here it's more personal, more real. This happened—but how could it? His long pause after 'playing' points up the internal rhyme with 'saying,' but more important, underlines the isolation of 'solitaire.' Then a smaller catch squeezes unsettlingly between 'un-' and an uneasily stretched out, tonally wavering 'easy.'

"He then eases into the long 'ee' of 'easy chair,' both caressing and bending the note so that it captures not only the seductiveness of the chair, that haven of comfort it never occurred to him he could lose, but also his current squirm of discomfort, ache of regret. The wry wordplay makes the immensity of this loss somehow both more and less bearable. As the poet Elizabeth Bishop wrote, with merciless self-irony, sharing with Lorenz Hart her 'one art,' the attempt to keep despair at bay through writing: 'The art of losing isn't hard to master.' Sinatra has always been a master of that art."

"WHETHER THE LYRICS were magical or hackneyed, most songwriting teams obeyed the romantic conventions of the time: the door closes before things really get sticky. In Frank's versions, the music expresses the unspoken details.

"Even when recording the finest compositions, the singer makes minute but crucial decisions that place his mark on the song. Take Rodgers & Hart's 'Dancing on the Ceiling.' I imagine it was written as a whimsical fantasy number, with a clipped 1930s dance rhythm. Sinatra adds one crucial word to the lyric—the 'all' in 'all through the night'—and drags out the thought to give it a real sense of longing. The concentrated meaning he brings to certain lines transforms a polite and charming song into something visual and erotic."

—Elvis Costello, *Mojo* (July 1998)

THE CHAIRMAN OF the Board hired Gene Kelly to direct the last of the musical Rat Pack pics: *Robin and the Seven Hoods*, which adapted the Robin Hood story to the specifics of Chicagoland mobsters in the 1930s and added songs by Jimmy Van Heusen and Sammy Cahn. Filming took place in 1963, but the assassination of President Kennedy on November 22 and the kidnapping of Sinatra's son two weeks later took the joy out of it.

It was Gene who had taught Francis Albert to dance well enough to partner with him in three musical movies, back in the late 1940s, when Frank was game for anything. A champion of modern dance as a narrative component in motion pictures as ambitious and accomplished as *An American in Paris* and *It's Always Fair Weather*, Kelly was a well-known perfectionist who would, when choreographing you, rehearse you until your feet bled. It was going to be fun working with Frank, Dean, Sammy, and Bing Crosby. It was going to be fun—until shooting was about to begin and Kelly realized that the guys were jaking it. Loafing. He was director in name only. So he quit.

Watch the dance done by Sinatra, Martin, and Crosby after they sing an ode to style in the *Mad Men* decade: "a flower's not a flower if it's wilted / a hat's not a hat till it's tilted." The singing's fine; the dance is fun to watch because of who the guys are, but it must be said: it's a sloppy performance. Kelly would never have signed off on it. "There are times in this business when you have to sit by a quiet lake and think about life," Kelly said after tendering his resignation. But the show must go on, and Kelly appeared with Sinatra in a 1973 TV special. Sinatra: "Did you watch those clips?" Kelly: "I watched my side of the screen." Sinatra (to audience): "This is the best friend I've got."

With the Basie band at the Sands.

John Dominis / Getty Images

69

WHEN I HEAR Sinatra sing "That's Life," I remember exactly where I was and what I was doing when he introduced it. It was the fall of 1966, and I was a freshman at Columbia University, reading Marxism for one course, Existentialism for another, Homer and the Greek tragedians for Humanities A, Plato and Aristotle for Contemporary Civilization, plus science (astronomy) and gym (tennis). I don't think it occurred to me that Sinatra was trying out a new, bluesy sound in "That's Life." With the girl chorus and the driving organ, he is in full Ray Charles mode, sounding a defiant blue-collar note. With the benefit of hindsight, you can see the song as a harbinger of the type of voter that put Republicans in the White House for twenty out of twenty-four years starting in 1969. But no one thought about that then. I loved the Everyman confidence of the song, which sounded personal even if you didn't know the rough outlines of Sinatra's career: *riding high one month, shot down the next, back on top in June*. As I was writing poetry and had begun to think of myself as a poet, I responded as much to the bravado as to the humorous p-popping alliteration in the line where Sinatra proclaims himself to have been "a puppet, a pauper, a pirate, a poet, a pawn, and a king."

Earlier in 1966, when I was still a senior at Stuyvesant High School, reading *The Lonely Crowd* and *Beyond the Melting Pot* in Advanced Placement sociology, *Esquire* came out with Gay Talese's famous article "Frank Sinatra Has a Cold," which opens with the brooding singer holding a glass of bourbon in one hand and a lighted cigarette in the other. Everyone else I knew was listening to the Beatles, the Rolling Stones, Bob Dylan, the Kinks, the Mamas and the Papas, and the Lovin' Spoonful. I liked them, too, but a singer born from another generation was singing the music in my heart. I was seventeen and went with Dennis Schoen and the Cohen sisters on a double date to see Julie Christie in *Darling*. A few months later, I saw *Blow-Up* in the movies and *Marat/Sade* onstage. I bought *September of My Years* and listened to "Last Night When We Were Young." It was a very good year.

70

AT THE 1998 Hofstra University conference devoted to serious Sinatra studies, Roger Gilbert of Cornell's English Department read his essay on "Sinatra and the Culture of the 50s."
One notion Gilbert pursues is that there are aesthetic parallels
between Sinatra and the Abstract Expressionists (or Action
Painters). "A moment ago I suggested that Sinatra might be
called a Method Singer; let me now propose that he be considered an Action Vocalist," Gilbert said. "Sinatra's best recordings, like his concert performances, always have the quality
of live events, of actions rather than mere recitations. Just as
we're continually aware of [Jackson] Pollock's choices, his split-
second swerves, hesitations and thrusts as he wields the brush,
so in listening to a Sinatra track we hear the impulsive gestures
of his voice as it carves its own path through a song. Improvis-
ing, ad libbing, bending or embellishing a melody, condensing
or stretching out a lyric, Sinatra is constantly making choices as
he sings, and that's surely where much of the excitement of his
music lies. There's a tangible riskiness in his best performances,
a willingness to leap without knowing exactly where he'll land.
As a result his records sometimes contain clinkers, clams, sour
notes, failed effects; but these stand as evidence of Sinatra's total
commitment to the moment in all its unpredictable power."
Later in the paper, Gilbert suggests that Sinatra is also a version
of Robert Lowell, a "Confessional Crooner."

The ad libbing, the word substitutions—sometimes unwise, sometimes terrific—lend immediacy to his performances. Seattle 1957, Australia 1959, Paris and London 1962, Caesars Palace 1982—fans know these and other concerts and treasure the variant live recordings of Sinatra standards. There are word substitutions in some of his studio recordings as well. "Ring-a-ding-ding, you're lovely" instead of "You know what? You're lovely" ("I Won't Dance"). Not "tear up" but "get rid of" your list ("Once in Love with Amy"). Not "you never can win. / Use your mentality" but "ain't no chance to win. / Why not use your mentality" ("I've Got You under My Skin" on *Sinatra's Sinatra*, 1963). Then there are the codas (or "tails") that end so many of his records: *You broke my heart, you took it apart, so pack up your baggage and beat it!* ("Why Should I Cry over You?"). *Let me say before this record spins to a close* ("Anything Goes"). And when the song is officially over, the postmortems: *And an Englishman is happy when he's fighting for his queen* ("A Foggy Day").

The songwriters did not necessarily approve. Cole Porter didn't appreciate "you give me a boot" in "I Get a Kick out of You." Ira Gershwin did not get a boot out of the insertion of "much" to modify "alarm" in his line about viewing the morning with alarm in "A Foggy Day." I have a feeling that Ira winced when he heard Sinatra mar an otherwise magnificent cover of "Someone to Watch Over Me" with the solecism of a dangling "but" in a clause beginning with "although." Frank Loesser, who worked with Sinatra on the movie version of *Guys and Dolls*, fought with him incessantly and wanted nothing more to do with the singer after the picture was wrapped.

71

SINATRA AFFECTED TO despise several of his monumental crowd-pleasers, such as "Strangers in the Night," which reached the top of the charts in 1966, and even "My Way," which at a concert he likened to the national anthem ("but you don't have to stand"). If you sang a song at every concert for years, he explained, you'd hate it, too.

Saddam Hussein may have been the world's most ardent admirer of "Strangers in the Night." In his palace days, Saddam played the song over and over. A longtime karaoke favorite, the song is less esteemed today than the song on the flip side of the 1966 45-rpm single, "Summer Wind." Though overshadowed back then, "Summer Wind" (music, Henry Mayer; lyrics, Johnny Mercer) is the one you'd want to build a movie around, as Stuart Rosenberg does in *The Pope of Greenwich Village* (1984).

For "Strangers in the Night," Frank couldn't resist a somewhat sarcastic little scat coda: *doo bee doo bee doo.*

Graffiti on posters in New York subway stations, circa 1966–67:

TO BE IS TO DO.——NIETZSCHE

TO DO IS TO BE.——SARTRE

DOO BEE DOO BEE DOO.——SINATRA

In March 1967, spring semester of freshman year, I was studying Rousseau in one class, *Paradise Lost* in another, and

Raphael in a third, when the great collaboration with bossa nova maestro Antonio Carlos Jobim was released. So big and brassy with Basie, Frank softens his voice in Brazil time. Accompanied by Jobim on piano, guitar, and backup vocals, he sings Jobim's "Meditation," "The Girl from Ipanema," "How Insensitive," and "Quiet Nights of Quiet Stars," the last of these with a lyric by Gene Lees. Maybe only Sinatra can sing a song ending "the meaning of existence, O my love" and get away with it.

Ava.

John Springer Collection / CORBIS

(72)

SINATRA MARRIED MIA FARROW in 1966 when he was fifty and she twenty-one. "I've got Scotch older than Mia Farrow," Dean Martin said. The marriage didn't take. One day he was telling Mia an anecdote about a technique he learned from Tommy and she interrupted to say: "Tommy who?" Is that when Frank knew? Years later Sinatra confessed he still didn't understand what *that* was about.

Parlor game: Which of the four Sinatra wives would you choose to be: Nancy Barbato, his first love, mother of his children, keeper of the family name and flame, to whom he was loyal though not faithful; Ava Gardner, perhaps the most beautiful brunette in Hollywood; the young Mia Farrow at the beginning of her career as an actress (*Rosemary's Baby*) and gossip-column stalwart (her subsequent consorts included Woody Allen); or Barbara Marx, who married him when he was "Ol' Blue Eyes," an institution, a legend, lingering on the stage for that rush of glorious adrenaline when he stood under the spotlight and heard the applause and the cheering. All but Ava Gardner survived him.

Keep a few images in mind—Nancy raising the kids and cooking spaghetti for the whole band; Ava in a leopard-skin maillot—and a few facts. In Sinatra's bachelor years, there were at least two, possibly three affairs that meant more to him than the marriage to Mia. And, when considering

Barbara Sinatra's material inheritance, you might modify it
by the knowledge that, according to Tina Sinatra's memoir,
Barbara was a greedy shrew, a gold-digging harridan, and a
major control freak resented and despised by the rest of the
clan in Sinatra's declining years.

73

SINATRA, WHO WANTED the role Brando got in *Guys and Dolls*, went on to record Sky Masterson's best song, "Luck Be a Lady," in 1963. He made it a key component of one of his hour-long *Man and His Music* TV specials. In both the Broadway show and the movie, Sky Masterson sings "Luck Be a Lady" just before the climactic throw of the dice on which everything rides: he will pay each gambler hard cash in exchange for "their souls"—their agreement to attend the Salvation Army meeting that will save the job of the doll he has fallen for, Sister Sarah. It is Sky Masterson's heroic moment. And Sinatra, desperate to sing it when the movie was made, got his chance ten years later when he made it a staple of his act.

The lyric fits him neatly: he is a dice player, forever wooing the muse of chance, confident that she'll reward him with a seven or an eleven. Surely this is how Sinatra wanted to be seen and understood as he negotiated that decade of unparalleled change, the 1960s, with its fundamental political realignments. When the period began, Frank was campaigning for the next president of the United States, who brought new vigor to the Democratic Party, new glamour to the political arena, and the "New Frontier" to Washington, D.C. By the time that period ended, Frank's closest pal in national politics was the recently elected vice president of the United States, Spiro T. Agnew, Republican from Maryland, scourge of the "nattering nabobs of negativism," in speechwriter William Safire's phrase.

With the Reagans at the Inaugural Ball.

Ron Galella / Getty Images

Why the shift? Perhaps, in part, because Sinatra's gamble on Kennedy had turned into a humiliation. He hated RFK and LBJ, but in the '68 race still stumped for Hubert Humphrey. He thought Nixon was "a bum," but came out for him in 1972. Old liberal Hollywood was stunned; Gregory Peck, Burt Lancaster, Warren Beatty, Shirley MacLaine wondered what had happened to their old liberal ally. So did Tina Sinatra, his younger daughter, who was twenty-four during the '72 campaign. Inspired by a Tom Hayden speech, Tina was working with Jane Fonda and Jon Voight on George McGovern's campaign when she heard what her father had done. Tina collected a speeding ticket in her huff. How could you do it, Dad? "That's the way it goes, kid— it's a free country." Tina says they agreed to disagree, but she came to appreciate that "from his own perspective" he hadn't really changed; he was still "an incorrigible maverick," who disdained a foolish consistency, "a patriot who proudly flew the nation's colors on his fifty-foot flagpole, but he was also the immigrants' son who believed in open borders."

Sinatra called the coin toss, and the coin came up heads and made him a winner. Richard Nixon prevailed upon Sinatra to come out of retirement in 1973 to sing at a White House state dinner for the prime minister of Italy. In the East Room, 220 guests heard "I've Got You under My Skin," "Moonlight in Vermont," "I've Got the World on a String." As an encore Sinatra sang "The House I Live In." After the applause died down, Nixon enthused, "Once in a while there is magic in this room." Frank was moved. At the gala for Ronald Reagan's first inauguration, Frank serenaded the new first lady with "Nancy (with the Reagan Face)." Sinatra also produced a one-hour TV special of highlights for ABC, and four years later he did it all again at Reagan's second inaugural.

The political transformation of Frank Sinatra from Roosevelt liberal (he boasted that he named his son after Franklin Roosevelt) to Reagan intimate reflects slights and favors,
friendships initiated or betrayed, but it mirrors as well a fundamental change in ideology and culture. What happened to
Sinatra's politics was not all that different from what a neocon-
servative such as Irving Kristol went through: the conviction
that the liberal ideals of their youth were not being served by
the Democratic Party. To some extent the change was genera-
tional. As early as the 1950s, Frank complained that rock-and-
roll music was "written and sung for the most part by cretinous
goons." A few years later Sinatra hosted Elvis Presley on his
TV show, but dressed him in a respectable tuxedo. The hippie
look was something else entirely. Sinatra never embraced the
rock-and-roll generation. And it meant that songwriting as he
knew it—and singing as he did it—was heading toward obso-
lescence. Out of date, out of mind. Frank covered a few Beatles
songs and other things he shouldn't have touched ("Winchester
Cathedral"), but he detested the ascendant taste in music, attire,
and comportment, not to mention the flag-burning excesses of
the militant left. Remember, this is a man who liked to conclude
his concerts with "America the Beautiful," inviting the audience to sing the line "God shed his grace on thee."

74

SINATRA TOURED THE world, giving concerts. He devoted the proceeds of some tours entirely to charitable causes. He gave large sums away. He would pick up the hospital bills of an actor friend in need—Lee J. Cobb, for example, when he had a heart attack in June 1955—and expected nothing in return. He was spontaneous. Once, on a visit to Gregory Peck's place, he saw an empty wall in the foyer. "You need a painting there, and I know just the one," he said. He went home and painted an abstract canvas for the spot.

Sinatra tipped (he called it "duking") more lavishly than anyone else. On the evening news if he saw some poor fellow whose house was damaged in a landslide, he might turn to an associate and say "Send him a nickel," meaning five hundred dollars. Every so often, when Sinatra did something stupid in public—throw a drunken tantrum, humiliate a reporter, make like an asshole—the fact would be reported to me, a known enthusiast, and one time I conceded the point but added that there were things he didn't get credit for: his many unsolicited acts of generosity and charity. Once, when I went into this rap with my wife, Stacey deadpanned: "Poor Frank."

After Sinatra died, on May 14, 1998, everyone quoted Dean Martin: "It's Frank's world, we're just living in it." When I told a friend, a very attractive and flirtatious woman of twenty-six, that I was working on a Sinatra obit, she said, "Is there a place in it for a photograph of me naked surrounded by Frank Sinatra CDs?"

The photo that dogged him for decades: Frank with Carlo
Gambino and associates, 1970s.

Fred R. Conrad / Getty Images

75

SINATRA HATED *The Godfather* and the Johnny Fontane character. Mario Puzo, who wrote the bestselling novel, incurred Sinatra's wrath for spreading the news that the mob had stepped in when his fortunes were bleakest and got him the role that resurrected his career. Because of *The Godfather*, to this day many people believe that Sinatra landed the part of Maggio in *From Here to Eternity* because a Mafia goon decapitated a stallion and put the bleeding head in the film director's bed while he slept.

At Chasen's restaurant in Hollywood the quick-tempered singer confronted Puzo. The author beat a hasty retreat, with Sinatra on his tail, screaming: "Choke. Go ahead and choke, you pimp." When the movie was released, Sinatra called the Johnny Fontane subplot a "phony story," and over the years there have been cleaner accounts of how it happened. We know that Ava Gardner lobbied hard for her husband, calling Joan Cohn, wife of Harry, head of Columbia Pictures. "I'll do anything," she said. "Just get him a test. He wants that part more than anything in the world, and he's got to have it, otherwise I'm afraid he'll kill himself." Besides, he was willing to do it for the minimum, eight thousand dollars total. He aced the screen test and peppered Fred Zinnemann, who directed the film, with cables signed "Maggio." Zinnemann was not unhappy when Cohn told him that Sinatra would play the part.

That is one story. Another has it that phone calls or visits of a threatening nature were made by Jimmy "Blue Eyes" Alo on orders from Frank Costello and Johnny Rosselli. And here again Harry Cohn's wife is cited as a source.* It is impossible to know for certain, if only because the law of "omerta," or silence, is reversed in the haze of recollection when an aging mobster may do a little bragging and make a reporter's day or a memoirist's hour.

The Mafia rumors made Sinatra see red. This was not the kind of publicity that he wanted or needed, and he was sensitive, too, to the plight of the stereotypical American whose last name ended with a vowel. He had been called a dago or a guinea or a wop often enough as a kid. He wanted to contest the prejudicial assumption that if you dig back far enough in an Italian-American's lifeline you will get to organized crime, though his own career did not make him an exemplary witness on this particular point.

Yet, for all his tirades and protestations, Sinatra confided to Francis Ford Coppola that he would have liked to play Don Corleone. He was offered but turned down the role of a senior Mafioso in *The Godfather III*. If it was the part played by Eli Wallach, the wheel would have come full circle: the role of Maggio was originally slated for Wallach.

---

*According to Kitty Kelley, *His Way* (New York: Bantam, 1987), pp. 203–13, Joan Cohn argued in favor of Ava's husband: "He's Italian and scrawny, so he'd be perfect." Jonie Taps, a Columbia vice president, also advocated for Sinatra. Taps said that Harry Cohn never owned a racehorse and was never coerced: "It just took a little needling . . . with a little help from Ava." The story, attributed to Joan Cohn, that the head of Columbia Pictures was visited by "two gentlemen from the mob" before deciding in favor of Sinatra is found in Anthony Summers and Robbyn Swan, *Sinatra: The Life* (New York: Knopf, 2005), p. 181.

76

RICHARD BURTON'S DIARIES reflect a vivacious intellect and brilliant conversationalist. Sinatra was a friend who could rub him the wrong way: "What a petulant little sod he is." Brando, too, could piss off the Welsh coal miner's son: Marlon "really is a smugly pompous little bastard." You get your phone call taken, he observed, only when he wants something from you. "Sinatra is the same. Gods in their own mirrors. Distorted mirrors." On the other hand, Dick will say this for Sinatra and Brando as well as for a very select few others (Peter O'Toole, Elizabeth Taylor, Jane Fonda, Barbra Streisand) and himself. We "carry something sanguicolous and the parasite is called 'press-envy.' " The reason: "We take risks and run against the conventional." I don't believe I have ever before encountered "sanguicolous" (meaning "living in the blood") in a sentence, which gives you an idea of Burton's vocabulary.

Burton recollects the night on Bogart's yacht, the *Santana*, when he and Bogey drank boilermakers (rye with beer chasers) while Sinatra serenaded Betty Bacall and whoever else was there for hours on end. When Frank endorsed Ronald Reagan's run for reelection as governor of California in 1970, Burton wrote, "That's like Laurel coming out for Hardy." Neither man "has had a thought of their own in their lives except about themselves."

Burton's considered opinion of Sinatra's singing, rendered in November 1971, was that he "interprets lyrics from common songs better than any of his rivals and is as I call him a fine interpreter of street corners poetry—one for my baby and one more for the road and other such good songs he can trick in such a way that they seem brilliant minor poetry." Burton can't resist adding that "when faced with something massive—like for instance *Hamlet*—[Sinatra] is completely bewildered." This is inadvertently very funny: "Sinatra can sing but he can't play Hamlet" is on a par with "Clayton Kershaw can pitch but Verdi is beyond him." But what is most extraordinary about the entry is the evidence that Sinatra, down on his luck in the early 1950s, asked Burton to read *Hamlet* with him "as he was going to make a comeback through the classics yet and he'd show the mother-fuckers."

Elizabeth Taylor chastised Burton the next day for sounding "very snobby about Sinatra."

When Burton died, in 1984—on August 5, the same day Marilyn Monroe died twenty-two years earlier—Maureen Dowd wrote the *New York Times* obituary for the "rakish stage and screen star." The Shakespearean stage actor was celebrated for "the Burton voice," among other qualities, Dowd wrote. With Liz Taylor, who married him twice—and to whom he gave a sixty-nine-carat Cartier diamond and other gifts equally lavish—he conducted a love affair as tempestuous as that of Ava and Frank. Liz dubbed Dick "the Frank Sinatra of Shakespeare."

TINA SINATRA ON her dad: "Had he been a healthier, less tortured man, he might have been Perry Como."

THE COMEDIAN DENNIS Miller joked about the turn in his politics after the atrocities of September 11, 2001. He was alarmed by how the rest of the world views "us." By "us" he means the United States. "I don't think of myself as a classic conservative," Miller said. "I think of myself as a pragmatist. And these days, pragmatism falls into the conservative camp. We have to depend on ourselves in this country right now because we can't depend on anyone else. We are simultaneously the most loved, hated, feared, and respected nation on this planet. In short, we're Frank Sinatra. And Sinatra didn't become Sinatra playing down for punks outside the Fontainebleau."

SINATRA IS THE godfather of the HBO series *The Sopranos*—arguably the most transformative TV series in the last twenty-five years. One season begins with Sinatra singing "It Was a Very Good Year." When Tony Soprano fingers an FBI informant, the fact that the suspect while in prison had made a bust of Sinatra proves vital. The mug shot of young Frankie in 1938 hangs on the wall in Tony's office at the Bada-Bing strip joint. When Tony's father, in a flashback, is in a merry mood, he dances with his wife in the kitchen, singing "All of Me," in the Sinatra manner, from the *Swing Easy* recording of 1954. The album *Sinatra's Sinatra* (1963) is visually conspicuous in another episode. In still another, Tony and Carmela Soprano are telling their children at the dinner table about the great contributions Italians and Italian-Americans have made to civilization. The list starts with Michelangelo and ends with Tony beaming: "and, of course, Francis Albert."

EVEN TODAY, FRANK Sinatra moves product. A senior corporate executive walks into a meeting with his chief subordinates, puts an eight-by-ten glossy of Sinatra on the table, and says, "This guy has been dead sixteen years and he still makes more money a year than all of us combined."

Back in 1988, Sinatra's cover of the Jerome Kern and Dorothy Fields classic "The Way You Look Tonight" (as arranged by Nelson Riddle in 1964) sold barrels of Michelob beer in a thirty-second spot in which the nocturnal Manhattan skyline is punctuated by the World Trade Towers like a pair of exclamation points. Sinatra, then in his early seventies, is casually dressed, sitting on a stool beside a grand piano, score in hand, warming up. The song swings; you see saxophones. But as we reach the mellow closure—the last line of the song ("just the way you look tonight"), repeated softly, tenderly—he is in his tuxedo, onstage. "The night belongs to Michelob."

In 2008, Sean "Diddy" Combs used "Come Fly with Me"—the title track from Sinatra's brassy Billy May–arranged album from 1958—in a commercial, shot in black-and-white, at one of the singer's California homes. Three years later, Diddy was back at it again with another "art of celebration" ad for Cîroc vodka. He assembled friends—actors Jesse Williams from *Grey's Anatomy*, Aaron Paul of *Breaking Bad*, Frank Vincent and Dania Ramirez of *The Sopranos*, Michael K. Williams of *The Wire*, and models Eva Marcille, Lisa Seiffert, Jessica White,

Jerica Lamens, Jing Ma, and Chrissy Teigen—in Las Vegas. It's the Rat Pack revived. The girls are at their foxy best; one of the guys wears a hipster hat. Vodka martinis are shaken, not stirred. Couples dance. Sinatra sings Frank Loesser's hymn to the gambler's creed, "Luck Be a Lady," from *Guys and Dolls*, as arranged by Billy May in the Reprise years.

Then there's Jack Daniel's, which Sinatra first encountered one sleepless night on Jackie Gleason's recommendation in the early 1940s. "It's been the oil to my engine ever since." He touted its salutary effects, praising "anything that gets you through the night, be it prayer, tranquilizers, or Jack Daniel's," to which he referred by name so often, and with such commercial benefits to the distillery, that *Newsweek* in 1965 reported that the grateful firm had awarded the singer an acre of ground in Tennessee. He kept a bottle nearby offstage, and he was buried with a flask of the sour-mash whiskey in his casket. In a commercial released last year, an announcer explains with cheerful morbidity that Jack and "the man" go way back: "They were inseparable. And as it turns out, they still are." Sinatra Select, at 90 proof, is selling at $175, and selling well, at twice the price of single-barrel alternatives that are at least as good, thanks to the ad and the name. Frank's recipe for punctuating the celebration called for "three rocks, two fingers, and a splash," the voiceover tells us. "So, Frank, here's to you." The last thing we hear is Sinatra's voice onstage: "That's the nectar of the gods, baby," he says.

81

E. J. KAHN, JR., wrote the first book on Frank Sinatra. *The Voice: The Story of an American Phenomenon* grew out of a series of articles Kahn wrote for *The New Yorker* in 1946. In 1977, Kahn decided to keep a daily journal, which was published in 1979 as a book, *About the New Yorker & Me*. I was curious to see whether and how Sinatra entered the diarist's consciousness thirty-one years later.

There are five mentions, and they fit together admirably: young Sinatra then; Sinatra and me; Sinatra and two young people now. On the basis of this evidence in 1979, a fortune-teller would have seen a bright future for the singer's reputation.

The first mention was prompted by Toots Shor's death in January. "The only time I was ever treated with civility, let alone courtesy, at Shor's, was when I had dinner there one night with Frank Sinatra while I was doing a profile on the singer. It was not the ideal setting in which to conduct an interview— the sidewalk outside littered with squealing bobbysoxers, and, inside, Sinatra surrounded by his usual retinue of flunkeys: press agents, gofers, and the omnipotent Mafia-type sidekick who functioned more or less as a bodyguard."

The second mention is the rueful recollection that his book *The Voice* didn't sell all that well, either because Sinatra's legions of fans were not book buyers or because the singer had not threatened to sue the author. Earl Wilson's "unauthorized biography" (1976) provoked such a lawsuit and "has done quite nicely."

The third mention is occasioned by the results of the mayoral primary in New York City. Kahn tells us he voted for the victor, Ed Koch, because his opponent, Mario Cuomo, was endorsed by Sinatra and Jackie Onassis.

The fourth is in the entry for November 13. An eavesdropping cabdriver hands Kahn and his companions a résumé, indicating he wants to perform for Frank Sinatra or his representatives, "due to my material being mostly his songs and his style, though I do not mimic him. I have been favorably compared to Mr. Sinatra and feel I would be ideal to play his role in any upcoming movie of his life story."

The last mention, ten days later, gets the least elaboration, but may be the most significant. Kahn gets a phone call from a young woman—his publisher has referred her—who is working on a doctoral thesis about Frank Sinatra. Many more such have been undertaken since.*

*E. J. Kahn, Jr., *About the New Yorker & Me: A Sentimental Journey* (New York: Putnam, 1979), pp. 65, 292, 354, 399, 406.

THE FIDELITY TO Sinatra on the part of certain disc
jockeys—William B. Williams, Sid Mark, Jonathan Schwartz—
is legendary. The last named, the son of composer Arthur
Schwartz, has been a passionate Sinatra aficionado from the
time he heard "The Birth of the Blues" as a teenager in the
early 1950s. Some years ago, on a Sunday afternoon, he played
a rare recording of Sinatra singing "Soliloquy" from *Carousel*.
It's an unusually long, musically varied tearjerker of a song in
which the character, a ne'er-do-well carnival barker, imagines
that the baby his wife is carrying will be a boy, enjoys the
thought, then realizes that it may be a girl and that "you can
have fun with a son but you've got to be a father to a girl," and
vows to make or steal the money needed for the child's upbring-
ing, or die trying. Sinatra gives it all he has. It's his birthday,
December 12, 2005. Frank has been dead now for nine years.
The song ends: "Or die." There ensues a hush. Then Jonathan
says, "I know you're listening," and I get the strong feeling that
he is talking not to the radio audience but to Sinatra.

"If you start with the fact that Frank is crazy, everything
else falls into place," Schwartz maintains. He may be right,
but I prefer Pete Hamill's way of saying the same thing—that
with Sinatra you have to remember that never, from the time
he was twenty-seven, did he know a day in which he was just
another guy rather than the most famous voice of his generation, who was used to having special entrances and exits,
bodyguards, an entourage.

THE TELEVISION DRAMATIZATION of Sinatra's life that his younger daughter, Tina, produced in 1992, starring Philip Casnoff, is excellent, in my view the best of numerous attempts to adapt Sinatra's biography, or aspects of it, to the little screen. Casnoff does an outstanding job of conveying Sinatra's physical presence, his moods, his body language. It is mainly Sinatra's voice coming out of Philip's mouth when he sings, though on a few cuts Frank Jr. substitutes invisibly for his old man. This is Sinatra's life as he would tell it, up until his return to Madison Square Garden for the Main Event in 1973.

WE'RE USED TO hearing from children of the famous who tell of being tormented and terrorized by their famous mom or dad. A celebrity with an adoring public is almost expected to have been a secret lush or a monster at home. Sinatra is the fortunate exception. His three kids display true filial loyalty and love and are unashamed to show it.

Frank Sinatra, Jr., who managed the tours his father made in his later years, can tell you exactly what Nelson Riddle brought to the recording of "Spring Is Here" on *Only the Lonely*, and to Frank's post-Presley foray into rock and roll, "Can I Steal a Little Love" in 1956. On a beautiful May evening a few years back, Stacey and I went to the Blue Note to hear Frank Jr., who was appearing with an octet that included a pianist, guitarist, trumpeter, trombone player, and two saxophonists. He did old favorites from his papa's repertoire: "Street of Dreams," and then the Riddle arrangement of "I've Got You under My Skin," "Summer Wind," "Luck Be a Lady," "Please Be Kind," and the Gershwins' "A Foggy Day." He told us that Riddle wrote the classic charts for "Under My Skin" in the back of the car on the way to the recording session—he was in a desperate hurry, having attended to three other songs that day. One of the most interesting details that emerge from the anecdotes he told was that he called his father "Sinatra."*

---

*There was a precedent for this habit. Frank's mother would refer to her

Tina Sinatra, the youngest of the kids, born in June 1948, eight days after I entered the world, has written a book about her father. In 2013, on Father's Day, Tina hosted a "Siriusly Sinatra" special in which she was joined by Natalie Cole, Monica Mancini (who tweeted excitedly about the "hen party"), Deana Martin, and Daisy Tormé, the daughters of Nat Cole, Henry Mancini, Dean Martin, and Mel Tormé. They told anecdotes about their fathers and played their songs.

Nancy, the eldest of the three Sinatra kids, has outdone the rest in filial joy and duty, from the time she commanded national attention with "These Boots Are Made for Walking" and collaborated with her father on "Something Stupid," a sweet and simple song that showed off her father's strengths and carved out a role for her as a natural harmonic partner. Nancy can never forget that she personally caused a song to be written and to join the ranks of the standards: "Nancy (with the Laughing Face"), with music by Jimmy Van Heusen and words by Phil Silvers. The song was originally written for Bessie, the wife of Johnny Burke, the lyricist who was Van Heusen's usual songwriting partner. The three of them, Van Heusen and Burke and Silvers, played it to such good effect that they repeated the act at birthday parties. When they sang it for little Nancy (with the necessary minor changes in the lyric), Frank was moved to tears, thinking Jimmy and Phil had written it for his baby girl. The trio never let on that the song had a different genesis. Jimmy assigned his share of the royalties to Nancy when Frank recorded it for Columbia in 1944.

---

son as "Frank Sinatra" even in his presence. "She wants to be sure that everybody knows who she's talking about," Frank laughed. See Earl Wilson, *Sinatra: An Unauthorized Biography* (New York: Macmillan, 1976), p. 343.

With Nancy Sinatra and kids.

Bettmann / CORBIS

On *Nancy for Frank*, her own regular program on "Siri-usly Sinatra," Nancy has advocated for a public statue of her father in Times Square. She points with pride to her father's enunciation—the clarity with which you hear each word that he sings. She would do combat with those who assume, from the gangster talk in *Robin and the Seven Hoods*, that that was how Sinatra spoke. "Now," she says, "I'm going to play my favorite cover of that Harold Arlen and Yip Harburg classic 'Over the Rainbow,' " and the voice you hear is not Judy Garland's from the movie but the ardent Voice of the early 1940s, supported by a girl chorus.

Following her father's example, Nancy names not only the singers of the cuts she plays but the songwriters and the musicians. And the way Nancy says goodbye at the end of a show is *echt* Sinatra. "Be safe . . . Think of our troops out there . . . and the ones who are missing. Sleep warm, Papa."

85

IN HIS MEMOIR *Music Is My Mistress*, Duke Ellington devotes a section to Sinatra, kicking it off with the observation that he is "a unique individual—a *primo* nonconformist *assoluto*." This is about as high a compliment as Ellington can pay. He speaks admiringly about Frank "as an artist" and about his commitment to race tolerance and his refusal to be bossed or tossed around. "He felt that a syndicated columnist had spoken out of turn. So what did Francis do? He slugged the cat, and then went on and upwards to still greater heights."

Sinatra seldom recorded songs by Duke Ellington, but when he did the results were breathtaking. In "Mood Indigo" (from the album *In the Wee Small Hours*), there is that grand moment when Sinatra delivers the word "no" eleven times, in the verse beginning "You ain't ever been blue." This is a saloon song par excellence: lonesome, intimate, yet not beyond the power of music to enchant: a wail modified by a sweet melody. Frank's other great Ellington cover is "I Got It Bad (and That Ain't Good)," on *A Swinging Affair*. The song is historically associated with the female voice and a specifically female predicament, which can be summarized in ten words: "I love the bastard even though he's a bastard."

Sinatra sang other songs that were generally associated with female performers: "Bye Bye Baby" from *Gentlemen Prefer Blondes*; "The Girl That Got Away," which had been "The Man That Got Away" when Judy Garland sang it in *A Star Is Born* but got a new, male-specific conclusion from Ira Gershwin at Frank's request; "I Could Have Danced All Night," Julie Andrews's showstopper in *My Fair Lady*.

His take on "I Got It Bad" suggests not only that the song is not as gender-specific as we had first thought, but also that the singer's expression of his masculinity includes a frank acknowledgment of a feminine side, a side that is vulnerable, gets wounded, hurts, cries, has his heart broken by a lover. It is a pity that there aren't more Ellington and Billy Strayhorn numbers in the Sinatra playbook. Ellington biographer Terry Teachout tells us that Sinatra tried to record "Lush Life," but that the song's intricate melody "defeated" him.

Between Sinatra and the Duke the respect was mutual. When Ellington unveiled his forty-five-minute jazz symphony *Black, Brown and Beige* at Carnegie Hall in 1943, it meant a lot to him that Sinatra came backstage armed with a bouquet of roses. And Ellington is one of the hundred notable jazz musicians who, according to Gene Lees, listed Sinatra as their favorite singer. The relationship as it unfolded between Ellington and Sinatra conformed to a familiar pattern: Sinatra, when he recognized musical genius, would seek to collaborate with the person or persons involved, would figure out ways to do so, and would respond with great generosity if and when misfortune struck the other. Sometimes the product was great: the albums he recorded with the Count Basie band swing in a way that transcends the time period. You can listen today to their "Fly Me to the Moon" or "The Best Is Yet to Come" and feel the immediacy of these songs in Quincy Jones's uptempo arrangements with lots of exclamatory brass. Sometimes the result was less memorable: the record Duke made with Sinatra in 1967, *Francis A. and Edward K.*, was, in Terry Teachout's words, "mostly lackluster," and Ellington makes no mention of it in the Sinatra chapter of his memoir, *Music Is My Mistress*.

In 1962, Ellington signed with Reprise, Sinatra's newly formed record company, saying he "thought it would be a very good idea to be contracted to some company which is controlled by an artist rather than a businessman. It gives the soul a better opportunity." When Ellington was ailing, Sinatra sent his private jet to Houston to fetch Dr. Michael DeBakey, then the most celebrated medical man in the nation, and bring him to New York to examine the Duke. When DeBakey said the situation was hopeless, Sinatra sent a steady supply of flowers and fruit to the Duke's hospital room at the Harkness Pavilion of Columbia Presbyterian Medical Center.

86

SINATRA AND PEGGY Lee liked each other a lot, and it is said—by Sinatra's former valet, George Jacobs—that they had sex as often as possible. We know that they had an affair, and that, after it ended, their friendship endured to their mutual benefit. Together they planned Lee's album *The Man I Love*, in 1957. It was her first album for Capitol Records—the prestigious label (founded by Johnny Mercer) with the image of the Capitol dome in Washington and the words "Capitol Records" in silver lettering against a black background. It was in the middle of Sinatra's great period at Capitol, and it produced a milestone in Lee's career. Sinatra chose the songs, wrote the charts, and conducted Nelson Riddle's orchestra. Two songs in particular stand out: "The Man I Love," the Gershwin standard in which "Tuesday" rhymes with "my good news day," and "The Folks Who Live on the Hill," the Jerome Kern and Oscar Hammerstein composition that became one of Peggy's signature songs. Lee quotes a music producer named Bill Rudman (who coproduced *Love Held Lightly*, her late recording of Harold Arlen rarities) on Sinatra and herself: "What we have here is Primal Masculine and Primal Feminine—yin yang to the max. And what deepens it is that Sinatra *also* had deep vulnerability and Peggy *also* had real toughness—all of which helped make their performances so rich. No wonder they were a mutual admiration society. They lived the whole blessed continuum of sexual energy."

Years later, when Peggy Lee was hospitalized in New Orleans, Sinatra sent his plane to pick her up and bring her to her house, where he had had an air-conditioning system installed.

87

SHECKY GREENE ENLIVENED his stand-up act with a story about the night Frank Sinatra saved his life. The comedian said he "was standing out in front of Caesars Palace one night and three big tough guys began to kick the hell out of me. They were giving me a terrible beating, but finally Frank came up and said, 'Okay, that's enough.' "

Brad Dexter, who played one of the good guys in *The Magnificent Seven*, saved Sinatra's life for real in 1964 when the two were in the cast of *None But the Brave* on location in Hawaii. On a beach day in May, Sinatra and the executive producer's wife, Ruth Koch, had swum out too far. They were fighting a losing battle with the waves. Thrashing in the water, their heads bobbing up and down, they were convinced they were drowning. "I'm going to die, I'm going to die," Sinatra screamed. Dexter swam out and saved them both. Stretched out on the sand, Sinatra had lost consciousness, and Dexter gave him artificial respiration. A few hours later, Dexter paid a call on Sinatra, who was on the phone with his daughter Nancy. The revived man, in bathrobe and slippers, fresh from his brush with the grim reaper, got off the phone and said to Dexter, "My family thanks you." This struck Dexter as a strange remark, "almost as if I had put him in the uncomfortable position of having to thank me for saving his life." No doubt, too, Sinatra now associated Dexter with an incident in which he did not necessarily behave with great courage; Dexter had witnessed his moment of weakness.

For a time Dexter was in Sinatra's inner circle, getting parts in one Sinatra enterprise or another. In the 1964 movie *Johnny Cool*, a curious little crime drama with a cast that included Sammy Davis, Jr., Henry Silva, Mort Sahl, Telly Savalas, Joey Bishop, and Elizabeth Montgomery, Dexter plays a gang boss who dies, ironically enough, in his Hollywood swimming pool when his house explodes. In *Von Ryan's Express* he plays the heroic American captain. Kitty Kelley quotes Dexter in *His Way*: "The Chinese say when you save a life it belongs to you forever. Frank would have much preferred performing the grand dramatic gesture himself and saved my life so that I would be the one who owed him and would be indebted to him for life, not vice-versa." Dexter had expected that Frank would be grateful just to be alive, but the night after the near-drowning, he came to dinner and witnessed a Sinatra meltdown. He took one forkful of the spaghetti pomodoro prepared by his valet, George Jacobs, "and then started yelling that it was not prepared properly. George stood there quaking in his boots, not saying a word as Frank seized the platter and threw the spaghetti in his face, screaming, 'You eat it. You eat this crap, I won't.'" Dexter witnessed other outrageous displays of temper and temperament and sounded off about them to Kitty Kelley. Sinatra had broken relations with him after the two worked on *The Naked Runner* (1967), Frank as the movie's star, Brad as its producer. The quarrels proved terminal. Years later, Sinatra would tell people that "an old guy on a surfboard" saved his life, not Dexter. Sometimes he said: "Brad who?"

As word went out about the near-drowning in Hawaii, messages came in from the faithful. Joey Bishop sent Frank a cable. "Did you forget yourself?" he asked. "You could have walked on the waves." Son of a gun.

88

AFTER THE ASSASSINATION of JFK, people felt sorry for Vaughn Meader. Meader specialized in imitating Kennedy's distinctive Massachusetts accent and got a hit record (*The First Family*) out of it. As of November 22, 1963, Vaughn Meader was out of work.

Sinatra's death in 1998 has been, conversely, a boon for Sinatra imitators.

In a few weeks, when I get back to the city, I am going to go to the Carnegie Club Cocktail and Smoking Lounge on West Fifty-sixth Street, which has just had a write-up in the *New York Times*. The patrons sample cigars—there are forty on the menu—and Steven Maglio, a tuxedo-clad Sinatra imitator, entertains. I will wear my new gray fedora. The *Times* reporter was impressed: with Maglio's "smooth croon, Rat Pack swagger and the benefit of a thick cloud of cigar smoke, listeners just might imagine they were at the Copa Room at the Sands in 1963 rather than one of the rare public places where you can legally smoke a cigar in 21st-century Manhattan." There is an eleven-piece orchestra and there are evidently "Sinatra groupies" who see the show every Saturday night at forty-five dollars a pop. "My biggest regret in life is that I didn't get to see Sinatra live," said thirty-six-year-old Jessica Kester. "When I come here, I close my eyes, and it's as good as really hearing him."

In June 2001, my wife, Stacey, took me to see another

Sinatra imitator, Cary Hoffman, on my birthday. When the musicians ramped up the original Riddle chart and Hoffman sang "I've Got the World on a String" with what seemed at that moment to be a pitch-perfect imitation of the original, I almost jumped out of my seat.

AT THE FIGHT of the Century, Muhammad Ali versus Joe Frazier at Madison Square Garden on March 8, 1971—which Frazier won by decision after knocking down the previously undefeated Ali with a tremendous left hook in the fifteenth round—Frank Sinatra sat ringside, photographing the bout for *Life* magazine.

IN 1997, A man accused of threatening to kill a former lover seemed to conduct himself according to the lyrics of Sinatra songs. Interviewed by a journalist in a diner, he sang variations on "My Way" to summarize his situation. On his former lover's answering machine he sang "This Love of Mine" in an attempt to reconcile. (Did he know that Sinatra himself had composed the lyrics to "This Love of Mine"?)

In season seven of *Mad Men*, the penultimate episode is set in June 1969. Peggy and Don are having a heart-to-heart about an ad she is supposed to create. Suddenly the familiar opening chords of "My Way" are heard. You hear it everywhere, she murmurs. It's on everybody's radio. And Peggy and Don dance as Sinatra sings. It's a way of telling time, a marker of the late sixties, proof of the show's verisimilitude. But it is also an important thematic marker: from that moment on, Peggy is hoping she will get to do things her way.

There isn't a made man anywhere who doesn't hold a special place in his heart for "My Way." Recorded on December 30, 1968, Sinatra's version sold well in the United States and possibly even better in the United Kingdom, where it spent seventy-five weeks in the top forty list.

In the Philippines, "My Way" seems to be the populace's karaoke song of choice, but you'd be a fool to sing it, because if you don't do it justice, you might pay for the failure with your life. There is a subcategory of Filipino crime dubbed the " 'My

Way' Killings." In 2010, the *New York Times* reported that the song had precipitated the deaths of at least six persons in karaoke bars "in the past decade." Why? Butch Albarracin, the owner of Manila's Center for Pop, an influential singing school, speculated that the macho lyrics lead to fights. Roland B. Tolentino, a professor at the University of the Philippines, pointed out that it "is a very violent society" and insists that "karaoke only triggers what already exists here when certain social rules are broken"—when somebody hogs the microphone, for example, or kills a much-loved tune because of a tin ear or a weak voice. The professor conceded, however, that the "triumphalist" qualities of "My Way" may play a part in the karaoke killings.*

"My Way" is not every Sinatra fan's favorite song. Rugged individualism is typically celebrated in the breach, not the observance, and this is rugged individualism squared. We protect ourselves with a coat of irony from our deepest, most passionate, impulses, and some cringe at the singer's shameless self-coronation. I understand these objections and recoil from "making it" narratives, but am sentimental enough that the song brought tears to my eyes on the day he died and again one day when I drove across the George Washington Bridge into the city and a CD of *The Best of the Reprise Years* was playing in the car. The quiet coda—"Yes, it was *my* . . . way"—is calculated to have that effect. This is Sinatra's song, ego, life. Who else could get away with such blatant self-mythologizing? No one else can sing "My Way" except in direct reference to Sinatra's treatment. This is true, for instance, of "Mein vayg" (Yiddish lyrics by Herman Yablokoff), the Barry Sisters' cover

*Norimitsu Onishi, "Sinatra Song Often Strikes Deadly Chord," *New York Times*, February 7, 2010.

on their 1973 album *Our Way*, and even the punk-rock version Sid Vicious did in 1978, parts of which you can hear in the closing credits of *Goodfellas*, as well as in a 2014 commercial for the Acura TLX.

So, then, here is yet another role for the born role-player to play, another episode in the life of this self-made nonconformist. He has been the boy wonder, almost terminally cute. He is the gum-chewing good buddy, and then suddenly he is the leader of the pack, the king rat. He has been the loner, the lover, the loser, three L-nouns that differ by only one letter. He is the playboy of *The Tender Trap*, the entertainer who overcomes adversity in *The Joker Is Wild*. He is the winking seducer on album covers: *Come Fly with Me*, *Come Dance with Me*. He is a flamboyant drunk, capable of outrageous behavior. Sometimes he goes too far, like the September night in 1967 when he threw an intolerable fit at the Sands in Las Vegas and got socked in the jaw by casino manager Carl Cohen and lost the caps off two front teeth. Now he is the gangster hero of the opera. "There were times, I guess you knew / when I bit off more than I could chew"—lines as if written for Sinatra, as if they applied to him and only he could do them justice.

You probably knew that the lyrics for "My Way" were written by Paul Anka. But perhaps you didn't know that the music is from a French song called "Comme d'habitude" (meaning "as usual") written by Claude François and Jacques Revaux in 1967. Anka, on holiday in the South of France, heard the former sing it and immediately decided to acquire the rights. After a dinner with Sinatra and cronies at which Frank said he was thinking of getting out of the business, Anka went to his IBM Selectric and asked himself, "If Frank were writing this, what would he say?" He tried to mimic the way Sinatra talked. "I'd never before written something so chauvinistic, narcissistic, in-your-face and grandiose," Anka recalls in his autobiography. "Everything in that song was Sinatra." Anka says he finished the song at five in the morning and immediately phoned Sinatra at the Las Vegas bar where he knew the singer would be. After he played the song, Sinatra said, "That's kooky, kid. We're going in." Anka: "Coming from Mr. Cool, that meant he was ecstatic."

91

DON RICKLES, WHOSE joke insults Freud would have had a field day with, kept Sinatra in stitches. When they bumped into each other, Frank would signify his enthusiasm by jovially exclaiming, "You fat Jew."

On November 12, 1976, Sinatra was Johnny Carson's guest on the *Tonight Show* when Rickles appeared, unannounced, and interrupted the interview with cheerful banter about Jersey gangsters with Italian surnames. Sinatra then told a "true story" about how he was eating at a restaurant one night when Rickles approached him. Don explained that he was sitting with a pretty girl whom he wanted to impress and would Frank consent to walk over and pay his respects? Sinatra agreed. But when he did as asked, Rickles brayed, "Can't you see I'm eating, Frank?"

Rickles could always get a rise out of the audience at the Sahara by launching jibes at Sinatra and his entourage. There were jokes about Jilly Rizzo, the Sinatra companion whose bar and grill was famously favored by Frank—and by certain mobsters. One night in 1970, Johnny Carson was at Jilly's at closing time, getting sloshed and making eye contact with a pretty brunette, who was, unbeknownst to him, a crime boss's *goomar*. Before the night was through, Carson got thrown down a flight of stairs, a contract was put out on him, and he retreated to his United Nations Plaza digs for three days, missing three shows, before the mess got cleared up.

Rickles to Jilly: "How's it feel to be Frank's tractor?"

Leo Durocher is next to be put down, and then the toupee-wearing Frank.

Gay Talese: "And when Sinatra laughed, everybody laughed, and Rickles pointed toward Bishop: 'Joey Bishop keeps checking with Frank to see what's funny.' "

Whatever else it was, the Rat Pack was a hierarchy, and there was always only one guy at the top.

92

IF DON DELILLO is to be trusted, Sinatra was a model for male behavior even when he was down and out. DeLillo's novel *Underworld* (1998) begins with the third game of the fabled 1951 three-game playoff series between the Brooklyn Dodgers and the New York Giants, hated interborough rivals—a game that would end with Bobby Thomson's three-run home run, giving the Giants the National League pennant, in what may have been the single greatest, and surely most lauded, moment in the history of our national pastime. In the stands are Sinatra, Jackie Gleason, Toots Shor, and FBI chief J. Edgar Hoover. Even though the game is played in the middle of Sinatra's famous slump, DeLillo describes him as "a reference for everything that happens. Somebody makes a nice play, they look at Frank to see how he reacts."

In the worst of times, when he had nothing else to depend on, there was always Atlantic City and his Italian-American core constituency. "Sinatra was down and out. I mean he was *out* of show business. Just out of the business altogether. He had friends in Atlantic City, though. He could always get work here, I guess. Or maybe he just likes the ocean, I don't know." The speaker is Roy Gerber, entertainment director of the Golden Nugget in 1982. "He loves this town, though. Always went out of his way to come here." One of Sinatra's bosom buddies was Skinny D'Amato, who owned the 500 Club, "and *that*, let me tell you, *was* a nightclub. . . . Before Sinatra got the part of Maggio in *From Here to Eternity*, that's all it was for him. Places like the 500 Club—*when* he could get work." Jonathan Van Meter picks up the theme in *The Last Good Time* (2003), his book about Skinny, the 500 Club, the Rat Pack, and Atlantic City. "The night of Frank's first show that August [1951], there were so many people on the street in front of the club that, for the rest of Frank's run, Skinny had to hire a dozen cops to control the crowds. 'It was like you were seeing the Messiah come to town,' said a waitress who worked down the street from the club. 'That's how he was to the Italians. They went crazy.' "

93

WHEN SINATRA RETIRED in 1971, Jack Benny visited Frank in the dressing room before his farewell performance and cracked up the understandably nervous singer by calling attention to his recent political about-face, extreme as it was. "This man endorses Ronald Reagan for governor of California. Now I would have endorsed Reagan quietly, but Frank did it first. So I come out second with a little endorsement, and what do I get from Frank Sinatra the next day but a one word telegram. It says 'copycat.' " Benny, master of the slow double-take and expert at timing, pauses. "Now *I* would like to retire, only"—sputter—"only, *I can't*." Then the two men talked comparative golf, and others (Cary Grant, Sammy Davis, Don Rickles) came to the dressing room to pay their respects.

Los Angeles, June 13, 1971. The audience included the Agnews, the Reagans, Henry Kissinger. Sinatra began with "All or Nothing at All" and, as if to review his career, "I'll Never Smile Again," "Nancy," "Ol' Man River," "I've Got You under My Skin," "The Lady Is a Tramp," "Fly Me to the Moon," and "My Way." He concluded his farewell with "Angel Eyes." The stage went dark, and he lit a cigarette. "Thanks to stagecraft and the majesty of his singing, Sinatra stage-managed a perfect coda," Will Friedwald writes. "As he delicately entered a diminuendo, the smoke from his cigarette gradually enveloped him as both the volume and the spotlight grew smaller and smaller. Finally, when Sinatra uttered the last line, "'Scuse me while I disappear,' he was gone."

After so perfect an exit, why did he return to the fray? Rosalind Russell, an old Sinatra friend, had the simplest and most convincing explanation. "He was simply bored," she said.

Lauren Bacall, a consolation for Frank in the wake of Ava.

Bettmann / CORBIS

WHAT WOMEN WANT (2000) is a passably watchable romantic comedy, but it does have a couple of moments of joy. Mel Gibson dons a fedora and dances to Sinatra's "I Won't Dance." Even better, Helen Hunt pops a cork to the strains of "I've Got You under My Skin." She sings along with Frank, dances too, and the song lives right through her, a bravura performance.

WHEN LEONARD FEATHER polled jazz musicians for his 1956 *Encyclopedia Yearbook of Jazz*, Sinatra garnered nearly half the votes for best jazz singer. He was named on fifty-six out of 120 ballots. Duke Ellington picked him. So did Miles Davis, Oscar Peterson, Carmen McRae, Horace Silver, Benny Goodman, Gerry Mulligan, Sy Oliver, Bud Powell, and Lester Young.

Miles in his autobiography: "I learned how to phrase from listening to Frank, his concept of phrasing, and also to Orson Welles."

It is not surprising that rap singers admire Sinatra's attitude for the same reasons that prompted Marvin Gaye to say that his "dream was to become Frank Sinatra": "I used to fantasize about having a lifestyle like his—carrying on in Hollywood and becoming a movie star. Every woman in America wanted to go to bed with Frank Sinatra. He was the king I longed to be."

THE NAME SINATRA contains, in anagrammatic form, the words sin, art, rain, tan, trains, stair, satin, saint, stain, Tina, artisan, rat, rant, strain, star.

BETTY JOAN PERSKE of the Bronx—that's Lauren Bacall to you—died this week. The daughter of Natalie Weinstein-Bacal, a Romanian Jewish immigrant, and William Perske, who was born in New Jersey of Polish parentage, Betty at nineteen taught Humphrey Bogart how to whistle in *To Have and Have Not* (1944). In the same film she sang the Hoagy Carmichael/Johnny Mercer song that Jacqueline Bouvier particularly liked, "How Little We Know."* Bogie was more than twice her age. He was smitten. The next year he married her. They starred together in *The Big Sleep* (in which she sang "And Her Tears Flowed Like Wine"), *Dark Passage*, and *Key Largo*. She played winningly in *How to Marry a Millionaire* and *Murder on the Orient Express*. She also had a distinguished stage career, winning a Tony for her performance in the musical *Applause* (1970).

After Bogart died of cancer in January 1957, Betty and Sinatra began an affair. They flew to Las Vegas for the opening of *The Joker Is Wild*. Sinatra proposed, but when word of the nuptials reached Louella Parsons and she reported it, Sinatra broke it off and froze Bacall out of his life. "Frank did me a great

---

*The future Mrs. John F. Kennedy, on her junior year abroad in Paris in 1950, wrote out the bridge of the song and translated it into French. See Alice Kaplan, *Dreaming in French: The Paris Years of Jacqueline Bouvier Kennedy, Susan Sontag, and Angela Davis* (Chicago: University of Chicago Press, 2012), p. 33.

favor," she told a reporter when her autobiography, *By Myself* (1978), was published. "He saved me from the complete disaster our marriage would have been. But the truth is that he behaved like a complete shit. Still, that was over twenty years ago. When I run into him now, we give each other a nice hello."

There was no love lost between Bacall and Ava Gardner. Ava: "Were you really going to marry her?" Sinatra: "Hell, no. I was never going to marry that pushy broad." Bacall: "I wish Frank Sinatra would just shut up and sing."

SINATRA DIDN'T LIKE to say that Jule Styne or Sammy Cahn or Dean Martin or whoever had "died." He would say they "had gone to the mountains." When Sinatra was contemplating his own trek up the mountain, those last few months, he wasn't always home. George Jacobs, his longtime valet, paid him a visit. "He said hello, and then 'Sinatra will be here any minute now.' "

He wasn't expected to last the winter of '97–'98. He suffered from bladder cancer, panic attacks, dizzy spells. Blood clots broke through the lining of his bladder. Passing them was agony. A blood transfusion helped. The hospital released him on February 12. It was only a matter of time.

When Sinatra reached the summit of the mountain, on May 14, 1998, they lighted the Empire State Building in his honor. "That's power," a friend said. "No," I said. "That's love."

"YOU DON'T KNOW Italians the way Italians know Italians," says jazz pianist Gene Di Novi, who was Lena Horne's accompanist. "Italians tend to break down into two kinds of people: Lucky Luciano or Michelangelo. Frank's an exception. He's both."

THERE IS, OR should be, an anthology of immortal epitaphs and choice standards for weepy moments at funerals. At the funeral of the painter Larry Rivers, who played saxophone and did a little singing, the mourners listened to a tape of Rivers singing "Everything Happens to Me." Willem de Kooning's biographers ended their Pulitzer Prize–winning book with a recurrent daydream that the painter had during his last years: "I would like to have Frank Sinatra's record 'Saturday Night Is the Loneliest Night in the Week' played at my funeral and imagine that all my friends' eyes should be drowned in tears." At Sinatra's funeral, the theme music of his radio and television shows was the obvious choice: "Put Your Dreams Away."

Emily Dickinson's epitaph is the suitably spooky "Called Back." Charles Bukowski's gravestone advises "Don't Try." Talk show host Merv Griffin opted for the witty "I Will Not Be Right Back After This Message." Jackie Gleason didn't have to give it a lot of thought: "And Away We Go!" On Johnny Mercer's gravestone, you will find the title of the lyric he wrote for a Ziggy Elman melody: "And the Angels Sing." On Jimmy Van Heusen's there's the image of a grand piano and the words "Swinging on a Star." Sinatra's final resting place bears the most optimistic of epitaphs, the title of the Cy Coleman/Carolyn Leigh song he made his own in the 1960s: "The Best Is Yet to Come."

Sinatra, snapping out of a haze,
noticed me sitting across from him
"Who the fuck are you?"
Just another fan, I said, on the day he died
I played "Close to You" and "Only the Lonely"
"Last Night When We Were Young"
and figured out my last message
I mean what I would say to him now
"your goodbye left me with eyes that cry"
on the other hand you left me the history
of your voice the record of the American century
from Roosevelt to Reagan you will live on
whenever I need to hear you (it has to be you)
sing "I Get Along Without You Very Well"
(Strand's favorite) or "I'm a Fool to Want You"
(my choice) when your lover has gone

Acknowledgments

Writing this book was a pleasure, but first it was a challenge. How do you write about someone who has provoked so many other writers, journalists, and novelists to erupt into prose? The decision to divide the book into one hundred discrete sections held the key. It followed from the knowledge that December 12, 2015, marks the hundredth anniversary of Frank Sinatra's birth. And it presented the writer with a flexible prose form—call it the *century*—that endowed an extra element of excitement to the composition of the book.

In limiting myself to "fair use" quotations from popular songs, I hoped to turn an obstacle into a formal requirement that is liberating to the precise extent that it is confining.

I want to thank Cal Morgan, my editor at HarperCollins, for his astute suggestions, exemplary attentiveness, and warm support throughout. I am grateful as well to Laura Brown and Joanna Pinsker of HarperCollins, and to my agents, Glen Hartley and Lynn Chu, of Writers' Representatives, Inc.

There are four others I would single out when accounting for the origin of *Sinatra's Century*. When she learned that not a day passes without my listening to Sinatra, Gillian Blake— who had been my editor at Scribner, publisher of my poetry— advised me years ago to write a book about my favorite singer. Richard Snow, editor of *American Heritage*, published a long essay of mine entitled "Frankophilia" back in 2002. I could not have written *Sinatra's Century* without the assistance of Stacey Harwood, my wife, who is my first reader and best adviser. Conversations with my friend Amy Gerstler inspired me, and it is to her that I dedicate the book.

About the Author

DAVID LEHMAN is a poet and writer. He is the founder and longtime editor of the *Best American Poetry* series and the editor of *The Oxford Book of American Poetry*. His *New and Selected Poems* appeared in 2013. His books of cultural criticism include *A Fine Romance: Jewish Songwriters, American Songs*, which won ASCAP's Deems Taylor Award; *The Last Avant-Garde: The Making of the New York School of Poets*; and *Signs of the Times: Deconstruction and the Fall of Paul de Man*. A core faculty member of the graduate writing program at the New School, he lives in New York City and Ithaca, New York.